With Love
for Franca
the sweetest of them all

'C— holds that a man cannot have a pure mind who refuses apple-dumplings.' – Charles Lamb

CONTENTS

CONTENTS

INTRODUCTION

Desserts have a long history. They go back to the beginnings of our civilisation. Take Melopita (p. 74), for example. This may well have been the Greek cheesecake to which Athenaeus, the author of *Deipnosophistai*, (*Specialists in Dining*), sang praises in the second century A.D. As is the way of many good things, cheesecake 'caught on' and is now a popular institution in many places, from Vienna to Florida, from Poland to Israel.

This ponderous beginning is to say that desserts are not the outcome of some modern frivolity, for great thinkers of the past, including Plato himself, liked to concern themselves with such questions of good eating.

In 17th and 18th centuries France, dessert was the one but last course of the meal and given elaborate presentation. These magnificent 'set pieces' in the words of Prosper Montagné 'owed more to architecture than to cooking'. An ostentatious array of these desserts was arranged to be consumed in a pre-determined order. It was followed by what was called *issue de la table*, a course of crystallised fruit and various preserves in syrup, etc. The mind boggles at their being able to issue from the table at all!

In our own time, the dessert is the final course of the meal and by shedding ostentation we have lost nothing in quality. We are much more sensible about what we serve to end a meal. A steamed or baked pudding is a very comforting end to a light meal in the winter. After a substantial meal, or on a busy summer evening, we may prefer a light sweet, an ice or an interesting fruit salad.

There is now a difference in the way desserts are served in France and in Britain. In Britain cheese is served after the dessert. In France the cheese is considered part of the dessert and is always served before the sweet, as it used to be in Elizabethan England. Shakespeare's dying John of Gaunt said :

More are men's ends mark'd than their lives before :
The setting sun and music at the close,
As the last taste of sweets, is sweetest last . . .

Some of the recipes in this collection may seem out of place, the cake section, for instance, but we have included them because they are served as desserts in their countries of origin.

There is a certain amount of overlapping and we have included variations when the difference seemed to us to justify it, as in the case of cheesecake, where country of origin is often disputed, but difficult to prove.

Another example is jalebis (p. 199), which is a favourite on Indian menus. In the course of research recently we came across a fascinating description of a mural inside the tomb of Rameses III, the last of the great Pharaohs of Egypt who built the Pavilion of Medinet Abu at Thebes, which depicts the process of making jalebis. In this early strip recipe the procedure is shown stage by stage and the name under which the ancient Jews and Egyptians knew this sweet was zalebi.

We were also excited to learn that the recipe for Indian gajjer halva (carrot halva) (p. 203) is known throughout the Middle East and the Hebrew name for it is gezzer halva.

The list of mouth-watering French desserts is endless. Their celebrated pastry has excellent flavour and texture and the extravagance incurred in providing the good ingredients is well worth it. On the other side of the scale, there are many delightful and economical fruit dishes and other desserts. The French house-wife is nothing if not thrifty and there is a lot to learn from her in the way of turning left-over plain, boiled rice or cake crumbs into imaginative sweets. We particularly recommend the tartlets, tiny cakes of ancient origin, known in the sixteenth century as flannets – diminutive of flan.

Britain has a great line in puddings and pies. We love to have gastronomically minded continental friends in Britain in the summer, so we can offer them Scotch salmon and an irresistible summer pudding to follow.

The Italians, who probably started what we call 'French' pastries, have many superb trifles, not least of them the zuppa inglese. What is more, they are responsible for introducing ices into Europe; some say from China, but Roman Emperors used to send runners to the mountains to gather snow, to be kept frozen well into early summer, in deep wells. The pulp of fresh fruit was served mixed with this snow for a very early 'ice'. Catherine of Medici with her Florentine cooks first took it to France in 1533. What a debt to owe a nation! They have also given the world zabaglione (p. 64) said to have aphrodisiac qualities. This bodybuilding 'custard' used to be served to new bridegrooms. Some waiters still cast a knowing eye over a young couple ordering zabaglione for two at the end of an Italian dinner.

German cooks have some exquisite creamy sweets. Just look at Bavarian creams. The Austrians adore sweet things and their desserts include delectable cream slices and strudels.

About the only good thing one can say about military conquests and colonisation – provided they are far enough away – is that they appear to bring in their wake a blossoming of exotic dishes. Most countries owe something to their one-time occupants. Without going so far back as the Romans, we can trace the arrival of sugar, rice and oranges in Spain with the Arab conquerors. To many today, an English breakfast without Seville orange marmalade is unthinkable. It was through Spain that chocolate first came to Europe from America. And that basis for innumerable sweets, sponge cake, also originated in Spain; the English name for it is a corruption of 'Spanish cake'. It is unusual for a normal Spanish meal, in an ordinary household, to end with anything but fruit, but for special occasions there are many exquisite desserts.

In Scandinavia the emphasis is on fruit and berries, especially in the summer season, with a lavish use of cream.

The Russians, too, are clever at using berries and cream cheese. They make excellent ice creams, which are so popular that they are eaten in the streets even in the winter. In *War and Peace* Tolstoy describes Natasha Rostov's birthday dinner and how she was persuaded to behave herself only after she was told that the Countess was going to have her favourite pineapple ice cream for 'afters'.

Hungarians like rich creams and cakes, which use practically no flour at all, but ground walnuts or almonds, and sweets served with thick chocolate sauce. They are all very good to eat and many have old-fashioned sexy names like 'Hussars' Kisses' and 'Love Potions'.

American sweets vary enormously, from substantial puddings to keep the pioneers' body and soul together to exotic pies and sundaes.

The Middle East provides many famous desserts and sweet-meats. Its inhabitants have a sweet tooth and whenever they can afford it, they gratify it with a splendid disregard for calories and expense. They are extravagant with cream, sugar, eggs and fruit. The Levant, with one foot in Europe and one in Asia, claims one of the oldest cuisines in the world. Turkish ekmek kadayif (p. 92), served with clotted cream called kaymak, is certainly a treat not to be missed. When well done, it puzzles all who try to analyse

11

the ingredients, believing them to be some exotic fruit. The ekmek is made of stale bread or shredded wheat biscuit, which has been used in Turkey for centuries. Desserts, as the West knows them, are not usual in countries of the Far East, though sweetmeats of all kinds are very popular.

In India there are many kinds of halva, made of carrots, beetroot, pumkin, marrow, semolina, bananas, eggs, mashed potatoes, etc., cooked with heavy syrup and decorated with almonds, walnuts, pistachio nuts, cashew nuts, raisins and cardamom. Halva can be served with a topping of double cream, whipped with a little sugar and a few drops of orange blossom water, then finished off with a sprinkling of almonds. Khir is Indian milk pudding, superior to the stodge which is often served under that name. For weddings and other festive occasions the Indians add to its opulence by decorating it with gold and silver leaf, silver balls, etc. A Kashmiri variation of this sweet is made of ground rice, and flavoured with rose water. Coconut delights (p. 198), are served in India as a special dinner dessert or as something for the ladies to nibble at tea-time. They are often decorated with blanched slivered almonds, crushed cardamom seeds, silver balls, silver hundreds and thousands, or, for a festive occasion, wrapped in silver leaf.

In Indonesia, as well as throughout Malaysia, gula malacca is a favourite dessert. It is about the only dish which reconciles me to sago. The best results are achieved with real palm sugar (gula malacca) but soft dark brown sugar will serve as a substitute. It is the two sauces served with gula malacca which make it so delicious.

The coconut features prominently in Filipino sweets and desserts. There is delicious buco, Filipino rice pudding, cooked with brown sugar and coconut cream; *buco pastelitos*, turnovers filled with flaked coconut, cooked with sugar, butter and yolks and brushed with cream before baking : there are bombones de buco – coconut fritters; coconuts flans and candy.

Desserts are practically non-existence in the Burmese scheme of things. There is a sago sweet and a semolina pudding, both made with coconut milk. A Burmese friend of ours makes excellent coconut fritters, using flaked coconut. A popular dessert is bananas in caramel syrup served with coconut cream, but by and large the Burmese prefer fresh fruit.

The Koreans too prefer fresh fruit to prepared desserts, but they have some interesting, highly calorific, sweetmeats guaranteed to keep out the cold. They also like compotes made of all sorts of fruit and berries, cooked lightly in water and sugar, or water and honey, syrup and served in individual bowls with a sprinkling of pine nuts on top.

The Japanese, apart from the Indians, are probably the most sweet minded people in the East. They contrive to make delicious and attractive looking desserts out of ordinary ingredients such as bean paste, sweet potatoes and chestnuts. There is a great number of very pleasant kanten sweets, based on kanten, a gelatinous seaweed, which enabled the Japanese to make jellies centuries before gelatine was invented. Certain desserts are reserved for special festivals. There is a two-coloured kanten or New Year jelly; plum blossom eggs for which the eggs are beaten with sugar and a touch of pink colouring, cooked gently, spread out on a board and stamped out into blossom shapes; and our own favourite, tangerine baskets, the recipe for which is included in the section on jellies.

No desserts are normally served in South China at ordinary homes or restaurants, except fruit or ice cream. In the North there are excellent apple or banana fritters, dipped in boiling syrup, sprinkled with sesame seeds then plunged in iced, cold water which crystallises the surface into crunchy caramel. In Szechwan the best known dessert is eight treasure pudding, an elaborate concoction of rice, mixed fruit, chestnuts and tousa– sweet bean paste. There is a wide range of Chinese preserves which are served with tea, after a meal. The best known of these are lotus nuts, ginger, kumquats and chow chow in syrup. Flavoured ices have been made in China since the earliest times and Marco Polo may well have brought back this art to the West.

ABBREVIATIONS

oz	–	ounce
lb	–	pound
gr	–	gram
kg	–	kilogram
ml	–	millilitre
dcl	–	decilitre

MEASUREMENTS

The ingredients are given in Continental, English and American weights and measures. These are not always straight conversions from the English measures, but suitable adjustments. Where, for the sake of convenience, 1 oz is shown as 30 grams, instead of 28.35, amounts of all ingredients have been proportionally scaled up or down. The cups, tablespoons and teaspoons are American Standard.

OVEN TEMPERATURES

Oven temperatures are given in all recipes in °C, °F and Gas Regulo. Allowances, however, have to be made for variations of settings on different models of electric cookers and it is advisable to consult the instructions supplied with the cookers.

Custards

BASIC CUSTARD CREAM

6 eggs
120 grs (4 oz or ½ cup) sugar
¾ litre (1½ pints or 3 cups) milk
1 teaspoon vanilla essence

⅛ teaspoon salt
¼ teaspoon cinnamon
a little grated lemon rind

Beat the eggs and mix with sugar. Scald milk and slowly add to the eggs. Before scalding milk, rinse the pan in cold water to prevent sticking. Pour into a double saucepan and heat (do not boil), stirring continuously for five or six minutes. Strain, add vanilla, salt, cinnamon and lemon rind, and chill. When grating lemon rind, grate the surface only, avoid the bitter white pith.

VANILLA CUSTARD

¼ litre (½ pint or 1 cup) milk
¼ litre (½pint or 1 cup) cream
1 small vanilla bean

4 raw egg yolks
120 grs (4 oz or ½ cup) sugar

Scald milk and cream with vanilla bean. Beat yolks with sugar in a double boiler and combine them with milk and cream, whisking vigorously. Cook over simmering water, stirring constantly, until it is thick enough to coat the spoon. Strain the custard and cool it, stirring occasionally. Custards can be variously flavoured by adding orange or lemon peel, chocolate, coffee, etc., instead of vanilla.

CALIFORNIAN CARROT CUSTARD

6 Servings
1 kg (2 lb) carrots
½ litre (1 pint or 2 cups) milk
4 beaten eggs
4 tablespoons honey

pinch salt
1 tablespoon soy flour
a little cooking oil

15

Scrub carrots well, cook in the minimum of water. Drain, cool and rub through a sieve or purée in a blender. Mix all the other ingredients and add to the carrots. Pour into oiled custard cups. Set cups in a shallow pan of hot water and bake in the oven preheated to 175°C (350°F or Gas Mark 3) for 40–50 minutes. Serve hot or cold.

CRÈME CARAMEL

4 Servings

90 grs (3 oz) loaf sugar	2 yolks
6 tablespoons water	2 whole eggs
½ litre (1 pint or 2 cups) milk	½ teaspoon vanilla essence
2 tablespoons castor sugar	

Cook loaf sugar with water without stirring until it acquires a caramel colour. This should be a good rich brown, not black. Pour into an ovenproof mould, or little individual moulds and tilt to coat all over. Leave to set.

Heat the milk to luke warm. Add sugar and stir to dissolve. Beat yolks and eggs together and pour the warm milk over them.

Pre-heat oven to 190°C (375°F or Gas Mark 4). Strain custard mixture into caramelised mould, put in bain-marie (a shallow pan of hot water) and bake for 40 minutes or until set. Leave until cold, turn out and serve.

SEVILLE ORANGE CUSTARD

6 Servings

1 tablespoon grated orange peel	4 egg yolks
1 tablespoon dry sherry	2 whole eggs
120 ml (¼ pint or ½ cup) orange juice	120 ml (½ pint or 1 cup) single cream
70 grs (2¼ oz or ½ cup) icing sugar	candied orange peel (p. 205)

In a bowl combine grated orange peel, sherry, orange juice, sugar, yolks and whole eggs, beating until nice and thick and smooth. Place this mixture over a pan of hot water. Heat the cream to boiling point and stir very slowly into the egg mixture, beating continuously until the mixture begins to coat the spoon. Pour into individual custard cups, cool and chill until set. Decorate with candied orange peel.

FILIPINO COCONUT CARAMEL CUSTARD

6 Servings

90 grs (3 oz or 6 tablespoons) dark brown sugar
2 tablespoons water
3 eggs
2 raw yolks

180 grs (6 oz or ¾ cup) castor sugar
small pinch salt
½ litre (1 pint or 2 cups) coconut cream (pp. 218–9)

Put brown sugar in a pan, moisten with water and cook until it forms a syrup. Pour some into six ovenproof cups, to form a good layer on the bottom.

Whisk eggs with yolks, castor sugar and salt. Gradually beat in coconut cream. Pour mixture into the cups, put in a bain-marie, bake in a very moderate oven, 175°C (350°F or Gas Mark 3) for about 40 minutes, until the custard sets. Run a knife around the edges of the dish, turn out and serve.

TEA CUSTARD CREAM

4 Servings

360 ml (¾ pint or 1½ cups) double cream
120 ml (¼ pint or ½ cup) strong china tea

120 grs (4 oz or ½ cup) sugar
3 egg yolks

Simmer the cream over low heat to reduce a little. Remove from the heat and stir in tea, sugar and yolks, beating constantly. Strain through muslin into four custard cups and put them in a pan of hot water. Cook on top of the stove until the custard is set.

CITRUS CUSTARD

6 Servings

4 oranges
6 eggs
240 grs (8 oz or 1 cup) sugar

juice of 1 grapefruit
juice of 1 lemon
4 tablespoons sugar for caramel

Grate the rind of one orange. Squeeze all oranges. Beat eggs and sugar until smooth, add orange rind and all the fruit juices. Mix well.

Pre-heat oven to slow: 150°C (300°F or Gas Mark 2). Caramelise a metal mould; heat 4 tablespoons sugar with 2 tablespoons water in the mould. As soon as the sugar turns light brown, tilt the mould so as to coat with it the bottom and the sides evenly.

Pour the custard mixture into the mould, stand in a pan of hot water or a bain-marie and bake in the oven until set.

Puddings

CHRISTMAS PUDDING

One 1–kg (2 lb) pudding serves 10–12

350 grs (10 oz or 2½ cups) flour
150 grs (5 oz or 1 cup) soft brown
   sugar
360 grs (12 oz or 1½ cups)
   shredded suet
1 teaspoon salt
240 grs (8 oz or 3 cups) soft
   breadcrumbs
1 teaspoon mixed spice
pinch nutmeg
240 grs (8 oz or 1½ cups) sultanas

240 grs (8 oz or 1½ cups) seedless
   raisins
240 grs (8 oz or 1½ cups) currants
240 grs (8 oz or 1½ cups) chopped
   candied peel (p. 205)
240 grs (8 oz or 2 cups) chopped
   blanched almonds
1 teaspoon grated lemon zest
5 eggs
¼ litre (½ pint or 1 cup) milk
3 tablespoons warmed brandy
1 teaspoon bicarbonate of soda

In a large mixing bowl, combine flour, sugar, suet, salt, bread-crumbs, spice and nutmeg. Mix all the dried fruits, almonds, lemon zest and add to the flour mixture. Beat the eggs, add all but 1 tablespoon of milk and stir well into the dry ingredients. Add brandy. Mix bicarbonate of soda with the remaining 1 table-spoon milk and stir well into the mixture. This amount of batter will make two 1 kg (2 lb) puddings, or one 2 kg (4 lb) pudding. For two puddings, butter two suitable pudding basins and divide the mixture equally. Cover with greaseproof paper and seal with aluminimum foil or a well tied cloth. Make sure no steam can escape from the puddings as they cook.

Fill two saucepans ⅓ full of water. When water boils, put in the puddings and cover. Boil for at least 8 hours. (For the larger pudding, boil for at least 12 hours.) To serve, unmould onto a serving dish, decorate with sprigs of holly, spoon brandy over the pudding, ignite and carry, in blue flaming glory, into the darkened dining room. Serve with brandy butter (p. 189) or cream.

KAISER'S PUDDING

4 Servings

30 grs (1 oz or 4 tablespoons) flour
½ teaspoon salt
75 grs (2½ oz or 5 tablespoons) sugar
2½ dcl (½ pint or 1 cup) milk

5 raw egg yolks
5 egg whites
60 grs (2 oz or 4 tablespoons) butter

Mix flour, salt, sugar and milk into a smooth batter, then beat in yolks. Whip the egg whites until stiff and fold into the batter. Pour into a round baking tin containing hot butter and bake for 15 minutes in a hot oven 220°C (425°F or Gas Mark 6), turn, and return to oven for a further 15 minutes to brown the other side. To serve, tear into pieces with fork.

EGYPTIAN BLACK CHERRY PUDDING

6 Servings

1 kg (2 lb or 5 cups) black cherries
30 grs (1 oz or ¼ cup) self-raising flour
4 eggs
⅛ teaspoon salt

60 grs (2 oz or ¼ cup) soft brown sugar
240 ml (½ pint or 1 cup) milk
120 ml (4 oz or ½ cup) cream
3 tablespoons butter
cinnamon sugar

Pre-heat oven to 220°C (425°F or Gas Mark 6).

Rinse and dry cherries, remove stalks and stone. Sift the flour at least twice. Beat the eggs thoroughly, stir flour and salt into them and beat hard. Sprinkle in sugar gradually, beating it in. Whisk milk and cream together and stir into batter, beat and blend thoroughly.

Butter an ovenproof dish, put in cherries, pour batter over them, put little pieces of butter all over the surface and bake for 30 minutes. Sprinkle with sugar flavoured with a dash of cinnamon and serve hot.

GURYEVSKAYA KASHA / RUSSIAN SEMOLINA PUDDING

6 Servings

½ kg (1 lb or 2 cups) chopped walnuts
10–12 bitter chopped almonds
¾ litres (1½ pints or 3 cups) cream
90 grs (3 oz or 7 tablespoons) semolina
a few drops of vanilla essence

120 grs (4 oz or ½ cup) sugar
¼ recipe short pastry (p. 181)
3 tablespoons full fruit jam
glacé cherries (optional)
3 tablespoons blanched slivered almonds
extra sugar, sieved

Pound the walnuts and the almonds in a mortar, adding a little water to bind into a smooth paste. Pour the cream into a shallow basin, hold under a medium grill and skim off the clotted top layers as they brown, putting them into a plate, until you have a plateful of this clotted cream. Put the rest of the cream into a saucepan, add semolina and cook a fairly liquid pudding (adding a little milk, if necessary). While it is still hot, add the nuts, vanilla essence and sugar and mix well. Butter a pie dish, line the rim with a little short pastry, put in alternate layers of clotted cream and semolina and teaspoons of jam, decorate the top with a few glace cherries and chopped almonds and bake in the oven preheated to 175°C (350°F or Gas Mark 3) for 35–40 minutes. When it has a crust on the top, sprinkle a thin layer of sieved sugar, covering the whole of the crust, put under a grill for a few minutes to glaze the top and serve.

WHISKY CHOCOLATE PUDDING
Very rich

6 Servings (or 4 for non-dieting gluttons)

12 sponge fingers (p. 127)	240 grs (8 oz) plain chocolate
3 tablespoons cold strong black coffee	5 eggs separated
3 tablespoons whisky	60 grs (2 oz or ½ cup) chopped roasted almonds

Arrange sponge fingers in a pretty glass serving dish. Sprinkle with mixed coffee and whisky so that the biscuits get pleasantly drunk without getting too sloppy.

Break up the chocolate into small pieces and melt very carefully in a basin, over a pan of hot water (not boiling). When quite melted, take off the heat and beat in the egg yolks one at a time. Whisk the egg whites to stiff peaks and gently fold into the chocolate mixture. Avoid beating. Pour mixture over sponge fingers and chill. Before serving, sprinkle top with chopped roasted almonds.

Brandy, or other eau-de-vie, can be used for this sweet, but we are rather partial to it with the whisky flavour.

CARIOCA TAPIOCA
8 Servings

1¼ litre (2½ pints or 5 cups) milk	3 tablespoons butter
2 tablespoons tapioca	1 egg
2 tablespoons Indian meal	1 teaspoon salt
240 grs (8 oz or ⅔ cup) molasses	1 teaspoon ginger
90 grs (3 oz or 6 tablespoons) sugar	

Scald ½ litre (1 pint or 2 cups) of milk. Mix together tapioca, Indian meal, molasses and sugar and stir into the hot milk. Cook for 15–20 minutes, stirring all the time, until the mixture thickens. Remove from heat. Add another ½ litre (1 pint or 2 cups) milk, butter, egg, salt and ginger to the mixture, stir and pour into a buttered baking dish set in a pan of hot water. Bake in the oven pre-heated to 175°C (350°F or Gas Mark 3) for 3 hours. Add remaining milk and cook for another hour. Do not stir. Serve with whipped cream (p. 189) or rum butter (p. 189).

QUEEN OF PUDDING (ENGLISH TRADITIONAL)

6 Servings

2 slices of bread
½ litre (1 pint or 2 cups) milk
2 eggs separated
grated rind of ½ lemon
1 tablespoon butter

120 grs (4 oz or ½ cup) vanilla castor sugar (p. 113)
4 tablespoons granulated sugar
2 tablespoons dessicated coconut

Cut the bread into cubes. Heat milk to scalding point and pour over bread. Rub through a sieve or pass through a blender. Add lightly beaten yolks, lemon rind, butter and vanilla sugar. Put mixture in buttered baking pan and bake in the oven pre-heated to 175°C (350°F or Gas Mark 3) for an hour, or until done. Beat egg whites until fluffy, add granulated sugar, beating until the whites form stiff peaks. Fold in coconut. Spread evenly over pudding. Brown top under the grill or in a hot oven and serve hot.

CABINET PUDDING

6 Servings

½ litre (1 pint or 2 cups) milk
30 grs (1 oz or 2 tablespoons) sugar
30 grs (1 oz or 2 tablespoons) butter

180 grs (6 oz or 2 cups) cake crumbs
2 eggs
⅛ teaspoon salt
1 teaspoon vanilla

In a saucepan, combine milk, sugar and butter. Cook over a low heat until scalding point. Do not boil. Cool. Add cake crumbs to the milk. Beat the eggs, salt and vanilla into them and add to the mixture. Pour into a buttered 1 litre (1 quart) ovenproof dish and set in a pan of hot water. Bake in the oven pre-heated to 190°C (375°F or Gas Mark 4) for 45 minutes.

EARLY PIONEER YAM PUDDING

10 Servings

120 grs (4 oz or ½ cup) sugar
120 grs (4 oz or ½ cup) butter
120 grs (4 oz or ½ cup) finely
    chopped nuts
3 eggs
1 kg (2 lbs or 4 cups) grated raw
    yams (sweet potato)

360 grs (12 oz or 1 cup) corn syrup
480 ml (1 pint or 2 cups) milk
1 teaspoon nutmeg
1 teaspoon cinnamon
1 teaspoon cloves

Cream together sugar, butter and nuts. Add eggs, one at a time, beating well each time. Add grated yams, syrup, milk and spices. Put into a well buttered casserole. Bake in the oven pre-heated to 175°C (350°F or Gas Mark 3) for 2 hours. Check pudding every now and then and if a brown crust forms on top, stir it in and continue to cook. If the pudding shows signs of drying out, add a little more milk. Serve hot with whipped cream (p. 189) on a very cold winter's day.

OLD FASHIONED MASSACHUSETTS OATMEAL PUDDING

8 Servings

1¼ litre (2½ pints or 5 cups) milk
6 tablespoons fine oatmeal
2 tablespoons butter
1 teaspoon salt
½ teaspoon ginger
½ teaspoon cinnamon

360 grs (12 oz or 1 cup) molasses
2 eggs
240 grs (8 or 1¼ cups) chopped
    apples (eating or cooking,
    according to the sweetness of
    your tooth)

Scald 1 litre (2 pints or 4 cups) of the milk in the top of a double boiler. Gradually sprinkle the oatmeal over the milk and cook for 15 minutes, stirring all the time. Add butter, salt, ginger, cinnamon and molasses. Lightly beat the eggs and add them to the mixture. Stir in the chopped apples and turn the mixture into a well buttered baking dish. Over all pour remaining milk. Bake in the oven pre-heated to 175°C (350°F or Gas Mark 3) for one hour. Serve with clotted cream or unsweetened whipped cream.

ALMOND PUDDING

4 Servings

1½ dcl (1½ gills or ¾ cup) milk
6 raw eggs yolks
60 grs (2 oz or 4 tablespoons)
    melted butter

30 grs (1 oz or 2 tablespoons)
    sugar
2 drops almond essence
2 tablespoons ground almonds
6 stiffly beaten whites of egg

23

Blend milk, yolks, butter, sugar, almond essence and almonds. Fold in egg whites, pour into a buttered baking dish and bake in a hot oven 220°C (425°F or Gas Mark 6) for 45 minutes. To serve, sprinkle with sugar and, using two forks, tear into portions.

SPANISH CHESTNUT PUDDING

6 Servings

500 grs (1 lb) chestnuts
¼ litre (½ pint or 1 cup) milk
4 tablespoons sugar
⅛ teaspoon salt

a few drops vanilla essence
4 raw yolks
4 stiffly beaten whites of egg
caramel (p. 217)

Split and boil the chestnuts in enough water to cover, for ten minutes. Shell, take off the skins and boil again in milk with 1 tablespoon sugar, the salt and the flavouring, until soft. Mash and rub through a sieve. Mix yolks with sugar, stirring thoroughly. Add the whites and mix with the chestnut purée. Line a pie dish with caramel, pour in the mixture, stand the dish in a pan of hot water, and simmer until done. Test with a needle; if it comes out of the pudding clean – it is ready. Cool and serve.

MATZO PUDDING

4 Servings

4–5 matzos
200 ml (7 oz or ⅞ cup) sweet red wine
60 gr (2 oz or ¼ cup) margarine
pinch mixed spice
120 gr (4 oz or ¾ cup) mixed dried fruit

90 gr (3 oz or 1 cup) roughly chopped walnuts
90 gr (3 oz or 6 tablespoons) brown sugar
2–3 eggs
2 tablespoons castor sugar

Put the matzos in a dish, cover with red wine and leave to soak just until they soften. Turn on oven to moderate heat 190°C (375°F or Gas Mark 5). Gently melt margarine. Lightly grease a baking dish. Mix spice, dried fruit, chopped nuts and brown sugar. Separate yolks from whites. Stir yolks into fruit and nut mixture. beat whites until very stiff. Put a layer of wine-flavoured matzo in the greased ovenproof dish, sprinkle with melted margarine, follow with a layer of fruit and nut mixture, and top with a coating of egg white. Continue in this manner until all ingredients are used up, finishing off with a layer of egg white. If there is any wine left over from soaking the matzos, spoon it over the pudding. Bake for 40 minutes. Sprinkle with castor sugar and return to the oven for 6–7 minutes.

Serve with Rum Sauce (p. 194) or Red Wine Sauce (p. 194).

DALMATIAN NOODLE PUDDING

4–6 Servings

180 grs (6 oz or 2 cups) fine
noodles
boiling salted water
1 jar raspberry jam

60 grs (2 oz or ⅔ cup) chopped
walnuts
3 tablespoons breadcrumbs
2–3 tablespoons butter

Cook noodles in plenty of lightly salted boiling water and drain.
Put a layer of noodles in a well buttered ovenproof dish, cover
with a generous layer of raspberry jam and sprinkle with walnuts.
Continue in this way, filling the dish with layers of noodles, jam
and walnuts. Sprinkle with breadcrumbs, dot with little pieces of
butter and bake in a very moderate oven 177°C (350°F or Gas
Mark 3) for 30 minutes. Serve piping hot.

CHOCOLATE STEAMED PUDDING

6 Servings
For Pudding:

3 tablespoons butter
165 grs (5½ oz or ⅔ cup) sugar
1 egg
270 grs (9 oz or 2¼ cups) flour

For Sauce:

60 grs (2 oz or ¼ cup) butter
240 grs (8 oz or 1 cup) vanilla
sugar (p. 113)

1 tablespoon baking powder
¼ teaspoon salt
240 ml (½ pint or 1 cup) milk
240 grs (8 oz or 1½ cups) plain
chocolate in pieces

⅛ teaspoon salt
120 ml (4 oz or ¼ cup) cream
2 tablespoons grated plain chocolate

Cream together butter, sugar and egg. Sift flour with salt and
baking powder, add to butter mixture, stir well. Add milk. In the
top of a double boiler, carefully melt chocolate and add to the
mixture. Pour into moulds, filling no more than half full. Stand
over a pan of water and steam for 2 hours.

Make the sauce. Work butter until soft. Add sugar and salt to
butter and mix well. Whip cream and fold into sauce. Pour over
unmoulded steamed pudding, sprinkle with grated chocolate and
serve hot.

NEW ENGLAND CRANBERRY STEAMED PUDDING

6–8 Servings

180 grs (6 oz or 1½ cups) crushed
cranberries
2 tablespoons butter
240 ml (½ pint or 1 cup) boiling
water

1 egg
120 grs (4 oz or ½ cup) sugar
180 grs (6 oz or ½ cup) molasses
180 grs (6 oz or 1½ cups) flour
1 teaspoon salt

Put cranberries and butter in a bowl, pour boiling water over them. Beat egg with milk, sugar and molasses and add to cranberry mixture.

Sift flour and salt together and stir into the mixture. Fold into a well buttered 1 litre (1 quart) mould, or pudding basin, and steam for 2 hours. Serve hot with cranberry sauce (p. 193).

CATALAN PRUNE PUDDING

6 Servings

2 dozen prunes	140 grs (5 oz or 10 tablespoons)
120 ml (4 oz or ½ cup) rum	sugar
3 yolks	½ litre (1 pint or 2 cups) milk
1 egg	1 tablespoon butter

Wash the prunes and soak them overnight in water with the rum. Cook the next day in the same liquid. Stone and rub through a sieve. Beat the yolks and the egg, mix with sugar and add milk and butter. Fold into the prune purée. Put into a pie dish lined with caramel (p. 217), and cook in *bain-marie* (a pan of hot water) in the oven, pre-heated to 175°C (350°F or Gas Mark 3) until done.

SUMMER PUDDING

All kinds of summer fruit can be used for this pudding; strawberries, gooseberries, blackberries, rhubarb, raspberries, blackcurrants and redcurrants, in any combination or a mixture of all. Some people gild the lily by using sponge cakes for lining the pudding basin, which seems a pity. Stale bread and blackcurrants or a mixture of ripe redcurrants and raspberries or loganberries make best summer pudding.

4–6 Servings

½ kg (1 lb or 3 cups) redcurrants	120 ml (4 oz or ½ cup) water
½ kg (1 lb or 3 cups) raspberries or	stale bread
loganberries	a few choice berries for decoration
150 grs (5 oz or 10 tablespoons)	whipped cream
sugar	

Cook the fruit with sugar and water until soft. Cut bread into slices about 1¼ cm (½ inch) thick, remove crusts. Line a pudding basin completely with bread. For this you may have to cut some of bread into little triangles, to make a mozaic to cover the bottom. The sides are simple to line – you cut the bread slices into fingers and fit them in all around. As soon as the fruit is soft, pour it hot into the bread-lined basin. Cover with a round piece of bread, press down with a plate and put a weight on top.

Leave to stand over night, by which time the bread will be completely saturated with the flavour and colour of the fruit juices. Chill, turn out on to a serving dish. If you have managed to reserve a few berries, decorate the dish with them. Serve with whipped cream.

Hot Desserts

ARMUT (PERSIAN PEAR AND MACAROON DESSERT)

6 Servings

6 pears
$\frac{1}{4}$ litre ($\frac{1}{2}$ pint or 1 cup) water
60 gr (2 oz or $\frac{1}{4}$ cup) castor sugar
$\frac{1}{4}$ teaspoon vanilla
120 ml (4 oz or $\frac{1}{2}$ cup) blackcurrant liqueur
$\frac{1}{2}$ kilo (1 lb) macaroons
500 ml (1 pint or 2 cups) sour
  cream

6 large eggs
180 gr (6 oz or $\frac{3}{4}$ cup) icing
  sugar
pinch salt
$\frac{1}{2}$ teaspoon oil
1 carton cream for whipping
1 dozen toasted, slivered almonds

Peel, halve and core the pears.

Put water, castor sugar and vanilla in a saucepan, slowly bring to the boil and cook gently until the sugar melts completely. Flavour with 1 tablespoon blackcurrant liqueur. Put the pears in a pan large enough to take them all. Pour the syrup over them, cover and poach very gently until tender. Remove from heat, leave to cool and drain.

Crush the macaroons in a bowl, sprinkle with liqueur, reserving 1 tablespoon for tinting whipped cream. Add sour cream, mix well and either rub through a sieve or put through a blender.

Pre-heat oven to 190°C (375°F or Gas Mark 4).

Separate the eggs. Beat the yolks with icing sugar and salt until creamy and pale coloured, add to macaroons and stir well.

Oil a 1 litre (1 quart) mould lightly.

Whisk the egg whites until very stiff, fold into the macaroon mixture. Pour the mixture into the prepared mould. Put the mould in a shallow pan of hot water and cook for 40 minutes.

Remove from oven and allow to stand while you whip the cream, adding the remaining liqueur to it, little by little. Unmould the baked macaroon mixture onto a serving dish. Surround with well-drained pears. Pipe or spoon a whorl of pink-tinted whipped cream into each halved pear, stud with slivered almonds and serve.

OEUFS A LA NEIGE

4–6 Servings
4 egg whites
180 grs (6 oz or 12 tablespoons) castor sugar
1 litre (2 pints or 4 cups) heated milk

½ kg (1 lb or 2½ cups) fresh sliced strawberries (or other fruit)
vanilla custard (p. 15)
1–2 tablespoons toasted slivered almonds

Beat egg whites until they are stiff, gradually adding sugar. Using a wet tablespoon, form the meringue into egg shapes and slip them off into simmering milk. Poach the meringues 2 minutes on each side, turning them once. Remove the eggs with a perforated spoon and dry on kitchen paper. Heap the strawberries in a dish, put the eggs on them, pour cold vanilla custard around the eggs, sprinkle with toasted slivered almonds and serve.

FLOATING ISLANDS

4 Servings
4 egg whites
pinch salt

4 tablespoons icing sugar
custard (p. 15)

Beat egg whites until stiff, with a pinch of salt. Little by little, incorporate icing sugar, beating it in thoroughly. Slip tablespoonful of the mixture on to the top of hot water in a shallow pan, bake in a moderate oven 190°C (375°F or Gas Mark 4) until light brown, then remove with a perforated spoon, arrange on a foundation of soft custard and serve.

TANSY (OLD ENGLISH RECIPE)

6 Servings
240 ml (½ pint or 1 cup) milk
1 dcl (1 gill or ½ cup) cream
pinch nutmeg
pinch cinnamon
3 eggs
3 whites of eggs
125 grs (4 oz or 1 cup) crushed biscuit crumbs
30 grs (1 oz or 2 tablespoons) butter

2–3 tablespoons spinach juice
1 tablespoon chopped tansy leaves
1 tablespoon sherry
1 tablespoon orange flower water
90 grs (3 oz or 6 tablespoons) sugar
pinch salt
1–2 peeled, thinly sliced oranges
extra sugar for garnish

Bring milk and cream to the boil, remove from heat, add nutmeg and cinnamon, stir to cool. Whisk in eggs and whites, strain and mix in biscuit crumbs. Add butter, spinach juice, tansy, sherry, orange flower water, sugar and salt. Stir to amalgamate, then set over low heat (preferably in a double saucepan over simmering water), simmer gently, stirring all the time until the mixture begins to thicken. Pour into a buttered dish and bake in the oven 149°C (300°F or Gas Mark 2) for 45–50 minutes, until well set. Turn out onto a heated serving dish, garnish with orange slices, sprinkle with sugar and serve. Serve a dish of cream separately.

SWISS CHERRY CLAFOUTIS

4 Servings

300 grs (10 oz or 2½ cups) sifted flour	3 egg whites
3 egg yolks	90 grs (3 oz or 6 tablespoons) sugar
⅓ teaspoon salt	½ kg (1 lb or 2½ cups) black cherries
milk	
1 tablespoon Armagnac	butter

Put the flour into a bowl. Make a hole in the centre and in it put the egg yolks and salt. Stir well, add enough milk to give a consistency of light cream. Add the Armagnac. Beat egg whites adding sugar gradually. Fold them into the first mixture and add cherries unstoned. Butter a deep pie tin and pour in the mixture. Dot surface with butter and bake for 30–45 minutes in the oven pre-heated to 175°C (350°F or Gas Mark 3).

FRIED CUSTARD CREAM

6 Servings

3 yolks of eggs	a grating of lemon rind
90 grs (3 oz or 6 tablespoons) sugar	½ teaspoon vanilla essence
45 grs (1½ oz or 6 tablespoons) sifted flour	1 beaten egg
1 tablespoon Madeira wine	breadcrumbs
½ litre (1 pint or 2 cups) milk	butter (or oil)
	icing sugar

Mix the yolks, sugar and flour. Add Madeira and slowly pour in the milk scalded with lemon rind and vanilla essence. Simmer gently, stirring all the time until the cream thickens, then cool. When the custard is cold and set, cut into squares, dip in egg and breadcrumbs, fry in butter; sprinkle with icing sugar and serve very hot.

EMPEROR'S CRUMBS

8 Servings

6 eggs
120 grs (4 oz or ½ cup) butter
pinch salt
120 grs (4 oz or ½ cup) sugar
180 grs (6 oz or 1½ cups) flour
2½ dcl (½ pint or 1 cup) milk

90 grs (3 oz or 9 tablespoons) sultanas
60 grs (2 oz or ⅔ cup) ground almonds
3 tablespoons vanilla flavoured sugar

Separate yolks from whites of egg. Cream half the butter, add salt and gradually beat in the yolks, sugar, flour and milk. Mix well. Add sultanas and almonds. Beat egg whites until stiff and fold into the mixture. Heat the remaining butter in a baking tin, pour the mixture into it and bake in a hot oven 220°C (425°F or Gas Mark 6) until the batter sets. Break up into small pieces with a fork, sprinkle with vanilla sugar and serve hot.

THAI SILK

4 Servings

300 grs (10 oz or 1¼ cups) sugar
240 ml (½ pint or 1 cup) water

1 teaspoon jasmine water
8 raw egg yolks

Slowly bring sugar, water and jasmine water to the boil, simmer gently until the syrup thickens.

Using an icing bag with a small nozzle or a narrow funnel, pour the yolks, a tablespoon at a time, into the syrup in the thinnest, thread-like trickle, and spiral them into little pyramids. As soon as these set, carefully remove to a heated serving dish. Cook a few at a time. Keep warm until all egg yolk has been used up.

The name 'Foi Tong' means literally 'String of gold'. The little 'spools' are piled on a small serving dish into a *wy*, a narrow pyramid, resembling the hands put together for a traditional Thai greeting.

POPPY SEED NOODLES

4 Servings

Home made egg noodles (p. 185)
90 grs (3 oz or 6 tablespoons) softened butter

60 grs (2 oz or ⅔ cup) ground poppy seeds
240 grs (8 oz or 1 cup) sugar
grated rind of 1 lemon

Boil the noodles in lightly salted boiling water, as described, drain well. Add butter and mix well to prevent the noodles sticking. Keep hot.

Mix sugar, poppy seed and lemon rind. Sprinkle over noodles. Shake to mix and serve at once.

Hot Fruit Desserts

BRANDIED GRAPEFRUIT

6 Servings
3 grapefruits	brandy
180 grs (6 oz or 12 tablespoons) demerara sugar	

Slice grapefruits in half, cut to loosen segments, remove seeds and inner skins. Spread 2 tablespoons sugar over each grapefruit and sprinkle with brandy. Let stand for half an hour, then arrange on a baking tray and bake in the oven pre-heated to 175°C (350°F or Gas Mark 3) until the top is bubbling. Serve very hot.

BANANAS MARTINIQUAISES

6 Servings
6 firm, ripe bananas	4 tablespoons sugar
butter	a large glass of rum

Peel the bananas and place them in a buttered shallow oven dish. They should fit snugly. Dredge with sugar and sprinkle with rum. Bake in the oven at 190°C (375°F or Gas Mark 4) until the bananas are tender.

BANANAS FLAMBÉE

4 Servings
6 bananas	45 grs (1½ oz or 5 tablespoons) sugar
90 grs (3 oz or 6 tablespoons) butter	3 tablespoons rum or brandy

Peel the bananas. Cut them in half lengthwise. Melt the butter in a pan and sauté the bananas for 2 minutes. Turn and sprinkle with sugar. When the sugar has melted, add rum and light. Serve immediately.

DANISH WINTER COMPÔTE

6 Servings

60 grs (2 oz or ½ cup) stoned
prunes
90 grs (3 oz or ½ cup) dried
apricots
45 grs (1½ oz or ¼ cup) sultanas
60 ml (2 oz or ¼ cup) sweet cider

2 bananas, sliced
1 tablespoon clear honey
120 ml (¼ pint or ½ cup) fresh
orange juice
2 tablespoons finely chopped
orange zest

Soak prunes, apricots and sultanas overnight in cider. Put into a
buttered ovenproof dish. Arrange a layer of sliced bananas over
the mixture. Mix honey with orange juice and pour all over the
top. Sprinkle with orange zest, cover and bake at 175°C (350°F or
Gas Mark 3) for half an hour. Serve hot.

APPLE INFANTA

6 Servings

6 apples, peeled, cored and sliced
180 grs (6 oz or ¾ cup) sugar
3 tablespoons rum
120 grs (4 oz or 1 cup) flour
3 lightly beaten eggs

60 grs (2 oz or 4 tablespoons)
melted butter
¼ litre (½ pint or 1 cup) warm
milk
1 tablespoon icing sugar

Sprinkle the apples with 2 tablespoons of sugar and rum and
leave for one hour. Mix the flour with the sugar, eggs and melted
butter, blend smoothly, add milk and mix well. Line a dish with
caramel (p. 217), pour in the mixture and bake in a moderate oven
190°C (375°F or Gas Mark 4) for eight minutes. Boil the apples
in their juice for one minute. Lay the apples in the dish in a
decorative pattern, replace in the oven and bake until the apples
are done. Do not over-brown. Allow to cool, sprinkle with icing
sugar and serve.

ALSACE APPLES

6 Servings

1 kg (2 lb) apples
210 grs (7 oz) butter
360 grs (12 oz) sugar
2½ tablespoons flour

375 ml (¾ pint 1½ cups)
milk
2 egg yolks

Peel the apples, core them, and cut in thin slices. Melt 150
grams (5 ounces) butter in a heavy pan and cook the apples gently
till almost tender. They should be pale pink and transparent.
Sprinkle with 240 grams (8 ounces) sugar and cook until the sugar

caramelises. Remove from heat and transfer the apples to a heatproof serving dish.

Heat the rest of the butter and stir in the flour. Add the milk and stir until you have a fairly thin sauce. Add the rest of the sugar. Remove from heat and cool to lukewarm. Stir in the egg yolks and spread the sauce over the apples. Bake for 30 minutes at 205°C (400°F or Gas Mark 5). Serve hot.

APPLES BONNE-FEMME

Allowing one per serving, choose large sound baking apples. Wash and core them.

Make a slight circular incision around the middle. Without peeling, put them on a buttered baking dish. Pour a few tablespoons water or white wine into the dish, fill the centre of the apples with sugar. Put half a teaspoon butter on each. Bake in a moderate oven 190°C (375°F or Gas Mark 4) for 25–30 minutes.

Arrange croûtons, fried in butter, on a serving dish and put an apple on each. (Sponge cake slices or madeleines (p. 87) can be used instead.) Pour a trickle of juices from the baking dish around the croûtons, sprinkle with sugar and coat with a little Kirsch-flavoured, half-set red currant jelly (p. 214).

CHINESE TOFFEE APPLES

6 Servings
4 cooking apples or 6 eating apples according to taste
Light batter (p. 185)

oil for deep frying
240 grs (8 oz or 1 cup) sugar
sesame seeds
a large bowl of iced water

Wash and peel the apples. Core and cut into bite-sized pieces. In a heavy bottomed saucepan, bring the sugar to caramel point (p. 217). Dip in batter, deep fry and drain. Drop apple chunks into caramel, stir to coat evenly and remove from heat. Sprinkle liberally with sesame seeds and serve. To serve, dip each mouthful into iced water before eating, to harden the caramel.

These should really be called caramelised apples, but in Chinese restaurants they are called 'Toffee Apples'.

BAKED ORANGES WITH COINTREAU

4 Servings
4 oranges
3 tablespoons sugar

4 tablespoons butter
3 tablespoons Cointreau

Cut the oranges in half. Remove seeds and pith. Sprinkle each half with sugar. Pre-heat oven to 205°C (400°F or Gas Mark 5).

Melt the butter and brush each orange half with it. Bake until the oranges are lightly browned. Spoon Cointreau over each one and serve at once.

APRICOTS COLBERT

6 Servings

300 ml (10 oz or 1¼ cups) milk
¼ teaspoon vanilla extract
small pinch salt
1 tablespoon sugar
4 tablespoons semolina
2 egg yolks
apricot sauce (p. 193)

Kirsch
12 apricots
1 beaten egg
1 tablespoon melted butter
white breadcrumbs
oil for deep frying
icing sugar
apricot sauce (p. 193)

Bring milk to the boil, add salt and vanilla flavouring, sweeten to taste and pour the semolina into it. Cover and cook in a moderate oven, 190°C (375°F or Gas Mark 4) for 30 minutes. Stir with a fork, blend in egg yolks, butter, and flavour with Kirsh.

Cook the apricots as described in the recipe for Apricot Compôte (p. 151), but do not cut them in half. Drain, half open them, remove pit and fill the cavity with semolina. Re-shape the apricots, dip them one by one in beaten egg mixed with melted butter, roll in breadcrumbs, and plunge into hot deep fat for about eight minutes. Drain on absorbent kitchen paper, sprinkle lightly with icing sugar, arrange in a pyramid, and serve with apricot sauce flavoured with Kirsch or Maraschino.

PINEAPPLE CONDÉ

6 Servings

1 pineapple
4 tablespoons sugar
120 ml (4 oz or ½ cup) Kirsch

dessert rice (p. 66)
apricot sauce (p. 193)

Peel pineapple and cut in half lengthwise. Remove hard core and cut into slices. Sprinkle with sugar and several tablespoons Kirsch and steep while dessert rice cooks. Turn hot rice out on to a serving dish and arrange the drained pineapple slices around it. Pour Kirsch-flavoured apricot sauce over the dish and serve.

PEACH CONDÉ

Peel the peaches, and prepare as indicated in the recipe for Pineapple Condé, but arrange rice in a ring. Finish off as described.

PEACHES FLAMBÉES

4 Servings

4 fresh peeled peaches, or 1 can peaches	240 ml (½ pint or 1 cup) syrup (p. 217)
	6 tablespoons Kirsch

Put the peaches and their syrup in a small saucepan with 4 tablespoons Kirsch. Heat slowly. Pour into a heated serving dish.

Heat the rest of the Kirsch and pour it over the peaches. Touch with a lighted match and serve immediately.

PEARS FLAMBÉES

As above.

PINEAPPLES FLAMBÉES

As above.

PEACHES IN ZABAIONE

6 Servings

6 peeled peaches	icing sugar
almond paste (p. 218)	zabaione (p. 64)

Cut peaches in half, remove stone and fill the peach halves with almond paste. Sandwich the halves together to reform the peaches.

Pre-heat oven to 175°C (350°F or Gas Mark 3). Arrange peaches in an ovenproof serving dish. Sprinkle with icing sugar to taste and bake for 15 minutes. Remove from oven, pour zabaione over peaches and serve at once. Alternatively, you can transfer peaches and their juices to individual parfait glasses, cover with zabaione and serve.

PLUM MIST

6 Servings

¼ litre (½ pint or 1 cup) red wine	4 egg whites
300 grs (10 oz or 1¼ cups) sugar	½ teaspoon vanilla
1 kg (2 lb) fresh stoned plums	

Gently bring wine and 240 grs (8 oz or 1 cup) sugar to the boil, stir until sugar dissolves completely. Add plums, cover, simmer for 20 minutes.

Pre-heat oven to 190°C (375°F or Gas Mark 4). Beat egg whites into soft peaks, gradually beat in remaining sugar and vanilla. Beat until meringue is stiff and glossy.

Transfer plums and their juices to an ovenproof dish. Spread meringue over them, bake for 13-14 minutes, and serve at once.

Cream Desserts

BAVARIAN CREAM

6 Servings

240 grs (8 oz or 1 cup) sugar
8 egg yolks
⅛ teaspoon salt
½ litre (1 pint or 2 cups) scalded milk
¼ teaspoon almond extract
½ teaspoon vanilla extract

1 envelope unflavoured gelatine
½ litre (1 pint or 2 cups) whipped cream
2 tablespoons confectioners' sugar
1 teaspoon almond oil
flavouring

Blend together in a double boiler the sugar, egg yolks, and salt. When the mixture becomes quite smooth, add scalded milk, almond and vanilla extract. Mix. Add gelatine, soaked in 4 tablespoons cold water. Keep the mixture on a low heat stirring all the time until it coats a wooden spoon. Do not allow to boil. Strain the custard into a bowl and allow to cool, stirring frequently. As soon as the custard begins to set, fold in whipped cream and confectioners' sugar. Add flavouring (coffee, chocolate, brandy, Kirsch, rum, lemon, orange, burnt almond, etc.). Coat a ring mould lightly with almond oil and put in the Bavarian cream mixture, filling the mould to the brim, pressing down lightly with the back of a spoon. Cover with a circle of paper and refrigerate for 2 to 3 hours.

To serve, dip the mould quickly into a bowl of warm water, dry it and turn out on to a chilled serving dish. Serve with small assorted macaroons.

You can fill the centre of the bavaroise with berries in season. Instead of being set in a mould Bavarian cream can be served in a glass dessert dish.

41

STRAWBERRY BAVARIAN CREAM

6 Servings

Bavarian cream (p. 41)
240 grs (8 oz or 1 cup) sieved
  strawberries
240 ml (½ pint or 1 cup) syrup
  (p. 217)

juice of ½ lemon
240 ml (½ pint or 1 cup) whipped
  cream (p. 189)
1 teaspoon oil
whole strawberries for decoration

Prepare Bavarian cream as described, using two envelopes of gelatine. When it starts to set, mix in the strawberry pulp and syrup. Add lemon juice and fold in whipped cream. Put into a lightly oiled mould and chill. Turn out on to a round dish and decorate with whole strawberries.

Apricot, pineapple, peach, pear, raspberry, lemon, orange and other fruit Bavarian creams are prepared in the same way.

DANISH RUM CREAM

6 Servings

15 grs (½ oz or 2 tablespoons)
  gelatine
4 tablespoons cold water
¼ litre (½ pint or 1 cup) double
  cream
360 ml (¾ pint or 1½ cups) milk
4 yolks

120 grs (4 oz or 8 tablespoons)
  sugar
⅛ teaspoon salt
2 tablespoons rum
whipped cream (p. 189)
grenadine liqueur

Soak gelatine in cold water, stir to dissolve. Heat cream and milk in a double saucepan over simmering water almost to boiling point. Remove from heat. Cream yolks and sugar until light and fluffy. Add salt and rum. Stir in 3 tablespoons hot milk, then blend in all the hot milk and cream.

Pour back into double saucepan and cook gently over barely simmering water, stirring all the time, until the mixture thickens enough to coat a spoon. Pour into six custard cups, cool and chill until ready to use.

Top with whipped cream, pour a spoonful of grenadine over the cream and serve.

CANADIAN MAPLE CREAM

6 Servings

1 tablespoon gelatine
2 tablespoons cold water
600 ml (1¼ pint or 2½ cups) milk
⅛ teaspoon salt

3 raw yolks
150 grs (5 oz or ⅔ cup) maple
  syrup
3 whites of egg
whipped cream (p. 189)

Soak gelatine in water for about 5 minutes. Scald milk in top of double boiler. Add gelatine and salt and stir until dissolved.

Stir a little of this mixture into the egg yolks. Add the egg yolks to the milk. Cook, stirring all the time, until the mixture thickens slightly. Cool for half an hour. Stir the maple syrup into the cooled mixture. Beat the egg whites until they form stiff peaks, fold into the mixture. Pour into individual moulds. Chill until firm. Serve with whipped cream.

BLACK TREACLE CREAM

4 Servings

7½ grs (¼ oz or 1 tablespoon) gelatine
3 tablespoons hot water
3 beaten egg yolks
2 tablespoons black treacle

½ litre (1 pint or 2 cups) single cream
3 egg whites
1½ tablespoons sugar
¼ teaspoon salt
2 teaspoons lemon juice

Dissolve gelatine in water. Mix yolks with treacle. Heat cream in the top of a double boiler, add sugar, stir until it dissolves. Pour cream gradually on yolks and treacle, blend well, return to double boiler and heat carefully over simmering water, stirring constantly, until the mixture thickens. Remove from heat. Beat whites with salt and lemon juice until very stiff, fold into the cream, pour into a dish, allow to set and serve.

ARABIAN NIGHTS CREAM

8 Servings

60 ml (2 oz or ¼ cup) dry sherry
1 tablespoon gelatine
½ litre (1 pint or 2 cups) double cream, whipped

3 tablespoons sugar, or to taste
12 crushed almond macaroons (p. 130)

Heat sherry but do not boil, pour over gelatine, stir until dissolved. Combine all remaining ingredients, add gelatine and mix well. Pour into individual glasses and chill. Serve with rosettes of whipped cream (p. 189).

PINEAPPLE LAYER CREAM

6 Servings

30 grs (1 oz or 4 tablespoons)
    gelatine
2 tablespoons hot water
2 tablespoons rum
½ litre (1 pint or 2 cups) milk
3 egg yolks
90 grs (3 oz or 6 tablespoons) sugar

1 vanilla pod
2 dozen sponge fingers (p. 127)
apricot or strawberry jam
diced ripe fresh pineapple, or 500
    grs (1 lb) tinned pineapple
½ litre (1 pint or 2 cups) whipped
    cream

Dissolve the gelatine in the hot water and rum. In a saucepan beat together the milk, egg yolks and sugar. Add the vanilla pod and heat mixture, whisking until it thickens into a custard. Mix in dissolved gelatine, remove from heat and leave to cool.

In a glass bowl place a layer of sponge fingers sandwiched together with jam. Spread with jam, which should be nice and tart. Add alternating layers of custard, pineapple, whipped cream and sponge fingers, in that order, finishing with a layer of cream. Decorate with a pattern of pineapple pieces. Chill and serve.

BANANA CREAM

4 Servings

4 ripe bananas
90 grs (3 oz or 6 tablespoons)
    unsalted cream cheese
2 tablespoons cream

5 tablespoons sugar
5 tablespoons redcurrant jelly
    (p. 214)
chopped almonds

Crush ripe bananas with a fork until smooth. Add the cream cheese blended with the cream. Mix well and add the sugar. Mix again and spread on a small serving dish. Cover with the jelly and sprinkle with almonds. Serve very cold.

KIRSCH CREAM

4 Servings

4 egg yolks
4 teaspoons Kirsch

60 grs (2 oz or 4 tablespoons)
    sugar

Cream yolks with Kirsch, mix in sugar, and beat until frothy. Pour into individual dessert glasses and serve very cold.

EGG WHITE CREAM

When you make mayonnaise or other preparation which needs yolks and have egg whites left over, here is a delicious way of using them up for an easily made dessert, which can be flavoured with 2 tablespoons fruit purée, vanilla, coffee, Kirsch, Maraschino or any other liqueur.

4 Servings
6 egg whites
240 ml (½ pint or 1 cup) milk

105 grs (3½ oz or 7 tablespoons) sugar
45 grs (1½ oz or 3 tablespoons melted bitter chocolate

Beat the egg whites stiff.

Scald the milk and add the sugar and chocolate, or whatever flavouring you wish. Combine the liquid with the egg whites and cook over heat, stirring constantly until thick.

LEMON BARLEY CREAM

4 Servings
½ litre (1 pint or 2 cups) barley water (p. 219)
6 raw eggs yolks
3 whites of egg

juice of 3 lemons
grated rind of 1 lemon
sugar to taste
orange flower water

Pour barley water into a bowl, beat in yolks and whites of egg, add lemon juice and rind, stir, sprinkle in sugar, blend well and simmer over boiling water, stirring constantly until the mixture acquires the consistency of cream. Strain, flavour with orange flower water and chill before serving.

SYLLABUB

6 Servings
480 ml (1 pint or 2 cups) milk
3 tablespoons sugar
2 eggs separated

grated rind of ½ lemon (½ orange)
240 ml (½ pint or 1 cup) dry sherry
grated nutmeg

Beat milk, sugar and egg yolks until smooth, stir in grated rind and sherry. Shortly before serving, beat egg white to stiff peaks and fold into the mixture. Pour into custard cups or glasses. Top with a little grated nutmeg. Drink happily.

Syllabub can also be poured over cake or used as a custard.

FROTHY SWEET YOGOURT

4 Servings
120 ml (¼ pint or ½ cup) yogourt
2 eggs, separated

2 tablespoons sugar
nutmeg or cinnamon

Warm yogourt in a double saucepan. Beat in the 2 yolks and cook, stirring all the time, for about 3 minutes. Cool. Beat the egg whites with the sugar to a smooth meringuey consistency and fold into the yogourt. Serve cold, dusted with nutmeg or cinnamon.

'INSTANT' COFFEE DESSERT

4 Servings

2 tablespoons instant coffee
milk
2 tablespoons confectioners' sugar

240 ml ($\frac{1}{2}$ pint or 1 cup) heavy cream
plain grated chocolate for decoration

Dissolve instant coffee in as little milk as possible. Add sugar. Whip cream and fold into the coffee and sugar. Pour into individual glasses and sprinkle with grated plain chocolate.

DRAMBUIE MOSS

4 Servings

a little egg white
granulated sugar
30 grs (1 oz or 2 tablespoons)
castor sugar
3 egg yolks

3 teaspoons lemon juice
4 tablespoons orange juice
2 tablespoons Drambuie
1 dcl (1 gill or $\frac{1}{2}$ cup) whipped cream (p. 189)

Dip the rims of 4 glasses first into egg white, then into granulated sugar to 'frost' them. Beat castor sugar and yolks until creamy, gradually whisk in fruit juices and Drambuie and cook in a double boiler over hot water until frothy. Cool, pour into prepared glasses, chill. Before serving, pipe a border of cream on top.

ZUPPA INGLESE

6-10 Servings

3 dozen sponge fingers (p. 127)
$\frac{1}{2}$ litre (1 pint or 2 cups) vanilla custard cream (p. 15)
120 ml ($\frac{1}{4}$ pint or $\frac{1}{2}$ cup) strong black coffee

120 ml ($\frac{1}{4}$ pint or $\frac{1}{2}$ cup) brandy
120 ml ($\frac{1}{4}$ pint or $\frac{1}{2}$ cup) liqueur
whipped cream (p. 189)

Divide the sponge fingers onto three plates. Sprinkle one dozen with strong black coffee, another with brandy, and the third with liqueur. Leave the sponge fingers to absorb the flavour. In a glass dish make a layer of the brandy-flavoured sponge fingers, spread with a third of the vanilla cream. Over this, lay the coffee-flavoured sponge fingers and a layer of vanilla cream. Finish with a layer of liqueur-flavoured sponge fingers and the rest of the vanilla cream. Top with whipped cream and chill.

Variations : Instead of vanilla cream, use bitter chocolate cream.

Instead of brandy, use white rum – instead of liqueur use a fruit syrup. (We have tried Ribena with success.) The final dish should have three different coloured layers with flavours that complement each other in a boozy way. No one has ever been able to tell us why the Italians call this trifle 'English Soup'.

DEVONSHIRE JUNKET

6 Servings
1 litre (2 pints or 4 cups) milk	1 tablespoon powdered sugar
1 tablespoon rennet	nutmeg
1 wine glass brandy or rum	Devonshire cream

Milk two pints of milk straight from the cow into a deep glass bowl. If you have no cow, buy milk as fresh as you can and heat in a saucepan to blood temperature.

Pour into your bowl and stir in the rennet and the brandy or rum. Place in a warm spot to set. When cold, sift sugar and a little grated nutmeg over the junket and cover with a layer of Devonshire cream.

OLD ENGLISH JUNKET

6–10 Servings
2 litres (4 pints or 8 cups) milk	clotted cream
sugar to taste	nutmeg
2 tablespoons rennet	

Warm the milk to lukewarm, stir in sugar and pour into a deep serving bowl. Stir rennet into the milk and put the bowl somewhere where it will not be disturbed until ready to be served. Just before serving, lay some clotted cream gently on junket. Grate a little nutmeg over the top.

COLD LOVE

6 Servings
Mixed fresh fruit (melon, pears, a bunch of grapes, oranges, pineapples, peaches, etc.)	4 yolks
	a pinch of cinnamon
180 grs (6 oz or $\frac{3}{4}$ cup) sugar	$\frac{1}{2}$ litre (1 pint or 2 cups) milk
120 grs (4 oz or $\frac{1}{2}$ cup) rum	2 leaves gelatine
	120 ml (4 oz or $\frac{1}{2}$ cup) cream

47

Peel and slice the fruit, sprinkle with 60 grs (2 oz or 4 table-spoons) sugar, sprinkle with rum and leave for two to three hours.

Prepare basic custard cream (p. 15) with 4 yolks, 120 grs (4 oz or ½ cup) sugar, cinnamon and milk. Dissolve gelatine in 2–3 tablespoons of warm water.

Mix the fruit with the gelatine and the basic custard cream. Stir gently. Whip the cream and add to the fruit, whisk lightly, chill and serve.

ASTURIAN CHESTNUT SWEET

6 Servings

Shell, boil and mash the chestnuts as for chestnut pudding (p. 24). Make a thick syrup (p. 217) and mix with the chestnut purée. Add the juice of 2 oranges and chill. Serve in a pyramid, garnished with slices of banana.

GULA MALACCA

6 Servings

water	pinch salt
240 grs (8 oz or 1 cup) sago	120 grs (4 oz or ½ cup) palm sugar
240 ml (½ pint or 1 cup) coconut cream (p. 218)	

Bring ½ litre (1 pint or 2 cups) water to the boil, add sago and cook, stirring, until the mixture thickens to a paste. Remove from heat and pour into a rinsed mould or into individual serving dishes. Leave to cool.

Now, proceed to make two sauces:

First, gently heat the coconut cream, season with a little salt and simmer until it thickens. Remove from heat, pour into a serving jug and leave to cool.

For the second sauce; cut up the palm sugar and put in a pan with 120 ml (¼ pint or ½ cup) boiling water. Simmer the syrup, stirring, until it thickens slightly. Remove from heat and allow to cool.

Turn out the sago as you would any jelly out of the mould or serve in individual dessert dishes. Pour some of each sauce over the gula malacca and serve.

CHESTNUT MONT BLANC

8 Servings

½ kg (1 lb) sugar lumps
2 vanilla beans
1 kg (2 lb or large can) unsweetened chestnut purée
60 grs (2 oz or 4 tablespoons)
   butter

480 ml (1 pint or 2 cups) double
   cream
120 grs (4 oz or ½ cup) vanilla
   sugar (p. 113)

Cook sugar lumps with 120 ml (¼ pint or ½ cup) water and vanilla beans until you have a syrup of soft ball degree (p. 217). Remove from heat.

Blend the chestnut purée and butter. Remove the vanilla beans and stir syrup gradually into the purée. Beat well. Force the mixture through a collander on to a serving dish in a mound.

Whip the cream and sweeten with vanilla sugar. Using a piping tube with a large nozzle force the cream around the edge of the dish and around the top of the mound. Serve very cold.

WHITE WINE DESSERT

4 Servings

4 eggs
180 grs (6 oz or ¾ cup) castor sugar
120 ml (4 oz or ½ cup) white wine

1 tablespoon (or 3 leaves) gelatine
2 tablespoons warm water
1–2 teaspoons almond oil

Separate eggs and blend yolks with sugar and wine. Cook mixture in a double saucepan over simmering water to heat and amalgamate it. On no account allow the mixture to boil. Remove from heat. Dissolve gelatine in water and blend into the wine mixture. Keep stirring the mixture from time to time as it cools, to prevent formation of skin on the surface. Leave until it begins to set. Whisk egg whites until very stiff, fold into mixture and pour into a mould lightly greased with almond oil. Chill to set. To serve, dip the mould into a bowl of warm water for an instant and turn out.

SAHALAB

This is a Yemenite milk dessert which resembles junket, except that cornflour is used instead of rennet.

4 Servings

1 litre (1 quart) milk
4 tablespoons sugar
4 tablespoons cornflour

3 tablespoons cold water
4 tablespoons ground coconut
cinnamon

Gently heat milk with sugar, stirring until the sugar dissolves completely.

Dilute cornflour with cold water, blend into milk and continue to heat on low flame. As soon as milk comes to the boil, remove from heat.

Pour into individual serving bowls, allow to cool then chill. Just before serving, top each bowl with ground coconut and sprinkle with ground cinnamon.

EGG-NOG GÂTEAU

10 Servings

7½ grs (¼ oz or 1 tablespoon) plain gelatine
4 tablespoons cold water
4 raw eggs yolks
1 dcl (1 gill or ½ cup) sherry
4 whites of egg

120 grs (4 oz or ½ cup) sugar
½ litre (1 pint or 2 cups) cream
1 teaspoon vanilla essence
½ kg (1 lb or 1 packet) sponge fingers (p. 127)
12 almond macaroons, crumbled

Mix gelatine with cold water, dissolve over boiling water. Beat egg yolks and gradually add sherry, stirring constantly. Add gelatine, mix well. Beat egg whites until stiff, add sugar, gradually, beating after each addition. Fold into yolk mixture, whip the cream and blend in half of it together with vanilla. Line a mould with sponge fingers. Fill the mould with layers of egg-nog mixture, sprinkling each layer with macaroon crumbs. Chill overnight. Unmould and cover with the rest of the cream, whipped into a foam.

Cold Fruit Desserts

HAWAIIAN PINEAPPLE SURPRISE

4 Servings

1 pineapple
240 grs (8 oz or 1 cup) cottage
 cheese

120 ml (¼ pint or ½ cup) cream
sugar to taste

Slice top off pineapple, hollow it out carefully leaving the shell intact. Finely dice the pulp. Rub cottage cheese through a sieve and add to pineapple. Whip cream and fold into mixed cottage cheese and pineapple.

Add sugar to taste. Spoon mixture into pineapple shell, replace top. Chill before serving.

WEST INDIAN PINEAPPLE

6 Servings

1 ripe pineapple
rum
3 egg yolks
180 grs (6 oz or ¾ cup) butter

4 tablespoons sugar
4 tablespoons toasted ground
 almonds

Peel the pineapple and cut into thin slices. Soak 1 hour in 120 ml (¼ pint or ½ cup) rum.

Stir egg yolks with butter in a double saucepan over simmering water until blended. Add the sugar and the rum from the pineapple, with all juice, and continue to stir until the sauce begins to coat the spoon. Remove from heat.

Drain the pineapple slices and arrange on a serving dish. Pour the sauce over the pineapple. Sprinkle with the almonds. Chill and serve.

INDONESIAN GINGERED PINEAPPLE SLICES

6–8 Servings

1 pineapple
juice of 1 orange
juice of 1 lemon
240 grs (8 oz or 1 cup) sugar

2 tablespoons white vinegar
60 ml (2 oz or ¼ cup) sherry
60 grs (2 oz or ¼ cup) sliced
    crystallised stem ginger

Choose a fine ripe pineapple. Peel and core it and slice in rings. In a saucepan, put the fruit juices, sugar, vinegar and sherry, stir until well blended. Add ginger. Simmer for 5 minutes. Add pineapple slices and simmer for a further 5 minutes, basting all the time. Chill and serve very cold.

BUTTER'D ORANGES (very old English recipe)

10 Servings

8 eggs
4 whites of egg
juice of 8 large oranges, strained
3 tablespoons rose water

240 grs (8 oz or 1 cup) sugar
2 tablespoons butter ('the Bigness
    of a large Nutmeg')

Beat the eggs and whites together, whisk in orange juice and rose water and strain. (The original recipe says: 'through a hair Sieve into a silver Bason'.) Add sugar, set over low heat or, better still, over a pan of gently simmering water, stirring all the time until the mixture begins to thicken. Blend in butter, decant into a flat dish and serve cold. 'It will not keep well above two Days, but is very wholesome and pleasant to the Taste.' It is, too.

ORANGES CHANTILLY

4 Servings

4 oranges
120 ml (¼ pint or ½ cup) double
    cream
60 grs (2 oz or 4 tablespoons)
    sugar

1½ tablespoons maraschino
4 tablespoons chopped walnuts
3 tablespoons orange juice

Cut off the tops of the oranges. Scoop out the flesh without breaking the skin. Save the juice and the pulp. Cut the pulp, free of seeds or pith, into small pieces. Whip the cream and mix in sugar, maraschino, orange pieces, walnuts and orange juice. Mix well and fill the orange shells with the mixture. Chill and serve.

CARIBBEAN MANGO DESSERT

6 Servings

240 ml (½ pint or 1 cup) fresh
  mango purée
2 tablespoons gelatine
300 grs (10 oz or 1¼ cups) sugar
6 tablespoons fresh lime juice
1 tablespoon grated lime rind
2 eggs

240 ml (½ pint or 1 cup)
  whipped cream
4 tablespoons orange juice
120 ml (4 oz or ½ cup) sweet sherry

Use fresh mangoes, peel and sieve or purée in a blender. Dissolve
1 tablespoon gelatine in 2 tablespoons cold water, stir. Put 180
grs (6 oz or ¾ cup) sugar, 4 tablespoons lime juice and rind into
the top of a double saucepan.

Separate eggs, add yolks to mixture in double saucepan, heat
gently over simmering water. Simmer, stirring constantly, until
the mixture thickens. Blend in diluted gelatine, remove from heat,
stir well and leave to cool. Beat egg whites until stiff. Fold the
whites and cream into mixture. Pour into a glass bowl, cool and
chill to set firm. Dissolve remaining gelatine in 4 tablespoons cold
water. Melt the rest of the sugar in 120 ml (4 oz or ½ cup) hot water,
add gelatine, mix well. Add remaining 2 tablespoons lime juice,
orange juice and sherry. Blend well, cool and chill until the
mixture half sets and becomes thick and syrupy. Carefully pour
over mango cream and refrigerate until completely set.

If fresh lime juice is not available, use lemon juice, but on no
account use bottled lime juice.

AMERICAN BLUEBERRY WHIP

6 Servings

360 grs (12 or 1½ cups) fresh blueberries
2 tablespoons sugar
2 eggs, separated

1 tablespoon unflavoured gelatine
½ litre (1 pint or 2 cups) fresh
  orange juice (or apple, or even
  pineaple)

Reserve 3 tablespoons fresh blueberries for garnish. Mix the rest
with sugar and let stand for an hour. Cook egg yolks with 360 ml
(12 oz or 1½ cups) fruit juice in top of a double boiler, stirring all
the time, until the mixture is just thick enough to coat the spoon.

Dissolve gelatine in remaining fruit juice and stir into the
mixture. Chill until it begins to set. Beat or whisk until light and
fluffy. Fold in blueberries. Beat egg whites until stiff and fold in

gently. Pour into a mould and chill. Unmould to serve and decorate with reserved blueberries.

The recipe can also be used with strawberries, raspberries, loganberries, blackcurrants, redcurrants, etc.

MRS SARAH HARRISON'S RASPBERRY FOOL

In 1743 Mrs Harrison suggested:

You muft have a Pint of Raspberries, fqueeze them, ftrain the juice with Orange-flower Water, put to it five ounces of fine Sugar, then put a Pint of Cream over the Fire, let it boil up, then put in the Juice, give it one Stir round, then put it in your Bafon, stir it a little in the Bafon, and when it is cold, ufe it.

Which is a perfectly usable recipe – and delicious. Only overshadowed, I think, by her Goofeberry Fool, which is fuper.

MRS SARAH HARRISON'S GOOFEBERRY FOOL

Take your Goofeberries, and fcald them very tender; then ftrain them off, bruise them very fine, and put them through a Sieve; let them be cold.

If a Pint of Goofeberries, you may add a Pint of Cream. Beat the Yolks of Eggs, fet it all over the Fire, and fweeten to your Tafte. Be fure to keep it ftirring till you think it will be thick enough, then put it in your Difh or Bafon.

FOR MORE MODERN FOOLS:

GOOSEBERRY FOOL

4 Servings

500 grs (1 lb) dessert gooseberries	120 ml ($\frac{1}{4}$ pint or $\frac{1}{2}$ cup) water
120 grs (4 oz or $\frac{1}{2}$ cup) castor sugar	120 ml ($\frac{1}{4}$ pint or $\frac{1}{2}$ cup) cream
	1 egg white, stiffly beaten

Stew the gooseberries and sugar in water until soft. Rub through a sieve or purée in a blender. Whip the cream until it will hang from the whisk. Add the stiffly beaten egg white and fold into the fruit purée. Pour into individual glasses and chill.

RASPBERRY FOOL

Follow above recipe substituting raspberries for gooseberries.

APPLE FOAM

6 Servings

Very good for slimmers. Choose nice sharp apples. We like Granny Smiths.

3 eating apples
lemon juice
3 egg whites
3 tablespoons clear honey

Wash and core apples, then carefully cut them in half and cut 2 neat, thin rings from each apple. Dip rings in lemon juice to preserve their colour. Shred the rest of the apples, skin and all. (No amount of lemon juice can prevent this from turning beige, but the final colour combination is very elegant.) Whisk egg whites until stiff, beat in honey and fold into the shredded apples. Pour mixture into individual glasses. Top each with apple ring. Chill.

PERSIAN MARBLE RHUBARB

6 Servings

500 grs (1 lb) rhubarb
2 tablespoons sherry
120 grs (4 oz or ½ cup) clear honey
240 ml (½ int or 1 cup) double cream
120 ml (4 oz or ½ cup) whipped cream
1 dozen small macaroons

Wash and string rhubarb, cut into little chunks. Cook it over low heat with sherry and honey, stirring frequently, for 10–12 minutes. Rub through a sieve or pass through a blender. Pour the rhubarb purée into a glass bowl, stir in double cream just to marble it without mixing too much and chill. Before serving, pipe a border of whipped cream and decorate with macaroons.

STRAWBERRY FROTH

6 Servings

500 grs (1 lb or 3 cups) strawberries
300 grs (10 oz or 1¼ cups) sugar
1 tablespoon brandy
360 ml (12 oz or 1½ cups) water
3 egg whites

Wash strawberries, cut in half lengthways, sprinkle with 6 tablespoons sugar and the brandy and leave for 2 hours. Over moderate heat dissolve remaining sugar with water to make a syrup. Rub strawberries and their juice through a sieve or purée them in a blender, adding all the syrup. Whisk egg whites until stiff, fold into strawberry purée and freeze.

STRAWBERRY CHARLOTTE

6 Servings

1½ kg (3 lb) strawberries
180 grs (6 oz or ¾ cup) vanilla
 sugar (p. 113)
2 tablespoons kirsch
360 grs (12 oz) sponge fingers
 (p. 127)

1½ dcl (¼ pint or ½ cup)
 maraschino
360 ml (¾ pint or 1½ cups)
 double cream, whipped

Hull the strawberries and cut them in half. Put in a bowl with half the sugar and the kirsch.

Moisten sponge fingers with maraschino mixed with equal amount of water. Line the bottom and sides of a charlotte mould with sponge fingers.

Put a layer of strawberries over the bottom layer of sponge fingers. Cover with a layer of the whipped cream, sweetened with sugar. Cover with moistened fingers. Continue in this way, finishing with a layer of sponge fingers.

Chill in the refrigerator. Unmould and serve with sweetened whipped double cream.

QUICK STRAWBERRY FLUFF

8 Servings

360 grs (12 oz or 2 cups) sliced
 fresh strawberries
2 egg whites
360 grs (12 oz or 1½ cups) sugar

4 tablespoons lemon juice
¼ litre (½ pint or 1 cup) double
 cream

Combine strawberries, egg whites, sugar and lemon juice in a bowl and beat with an electric beater until light and fluffy. Whip the cream and fold into the fruit mixture. Pour into individual glasses and chill.

PEARS WITH PRALINE AND TWO-COLOURED CREAM

6 Servings

6 dessert pears
240 grs (8 oz or 1 cup) sugar
¼ litre (½ pint or 2 cups) water
2 tablespoons Maraschino
1 tablespoon butter
1 tablespoon praline mixture
 (p. 218)

Sponge cake (p. 79)
Kirsch
120 ml (4 oz or ½ cup) raspberry-
 redcurrant jelly (p. 214)
whipped cream
a few drops vanilla

Peel pears, divide in half, scoop out core. In a saucepan, combine water and sugar and bring to a boil. Add pears and poach until tender. Put pears and syrup into a glass bowl. Cool and flavour with Maraschino. Chill. Mix the butter and praline.

Put the cake in a fruit dish, sprinkle with enough Kirsch to impregnate it thoroughly, spread with a thick layer of jelly, and put in the refrigerator for 10–15 minutes to solidify the jelly. Drain the pears and arrange in a circle on the cake. Put a teaspoon of praline butter in the centre of each pear.

Flavour half the whipped cream with vanilla and colour the other half a pale pink by adding a little half-set jelly to it. Using a forcing bag with a large fluted nozzle pipe the vanilla flavoured cream nearly all round the pears, then pipe a rosette of pink-tinted whipped cream in the centre of each pear. Scatter small rosettes of pink-tinted cream around the border. Serve with 'langue de chat' biscuits or tuiles (pp. 127–8). This recipe is equally suitable for peaches.

PEARS BOURDALOUE

4 Servings

4 large firm pears	4 egg yolks
360 grs (12 oz or 1½ cups) sugar	2 tablespoons flour
½ litre (1 pints or 2 cups) milk	3 tablespoons ground toasted
1 vanilla bean	almonds

Peel and quarter the pears and remove the seeds. Bring 1½ dcl (¼ pint or ½ cup) water and half the sugar to a boil and simmer the pears in the syrup for 15 minutes.

Bring the milk to a boil with the rest of the sugar and the vanilla bean. Mix the egg yolks and the flour. Remove the milk from the heat and pour into the egg mixture slowly, beating constantly. Put back over a moderate heat and cook, stirring constantly, for 5–7 minutes or until the mixtures thickens. Remove the vanilla bean.

Pour into a shallow serving dish and cool. Put pears on the sauce, and sprinkle with ground almonds, chill and serve.

REDCURRANT FLAMRI

6 Servings

½ litre (1 pint or 2 cups) white wine	2 eggs
½ litre (1 pint or 2 cups) water	6 egg whites, beaten stiff
180 grs (6 oz or 1 cup) fine semolina	1 teaspoon butter
300 grs (10 oz or 1¼ cups) sugar	150 grs (5 oz or 1¼ cups) red currants
⅛ teaspoon salt	2 tablespoons Kirsch
	candied cherries

57

Boil wine with water, gradually pour in semolina, mix and simmer gently for 20 minutes. Add sugar and remove from heat. Add salt, eggs and stiffly beaten whites, folding them in gently. Pour into a buttered mould, put in a pan of hot water, and bake in a slow oven 150°C (300°F or Gas Mark 2) for about half an hour, or until set. Cool. Turn out on to a serving dish.

Rub currants through a sieve, sweeten to taste, flavour with Kirsch and pour this purée over the flamri. Decorate with candied cherries.

STRAWBERRY CHANTILLY

4 Servings

½ kg (1 lb or 2½ cups) strawberries   120 grs (4 oz or ½ cup) sugar
360 ml (¾ pint or 1½ cups) double
   cream

Hull the strawberries, wash if necessary in cold water. Keep several of the largest strawberries for decoration. Force the rest through a strainer to extract the juice. Beat the cream stiff and sweeten with the sugar. Add 120 ml (¼ pint or ½ cup) strawberry juice. Divide the mixture in 4 goblets and decorate with reserved strawberries. Chill and serve very cold.

PEACHES NIÇOISES

4 Servings

4 large peaches   2½ dcl (½ pint or 1 cup) whipped
750 grs (1½ lb or 3 cups) sugar   double cream
6 tablespoons vanilla sugar (p. 113)   120 grs (4 oz or ¾ cup) wild
½ litre (1 pint or 2 cups) water   strawberries
3 tablespoons Kirsch   2 tablespoons slivered almonds
8 fresh ripe figs

Dip the peaches in boiling water and slip off the skins. Bring ½ kg (1 lb or 2 cups) sugar, vanilla sugar, and water to a boil. Put in peaches and simmer for 20 minutes. Remove the peaches to a shallow serving dish and sprinkle with 2 tablespoons Kirsch.

Peel the figs and force the pulp through a strainer. Cook in a saucepan with remaining sugar for 5 minutes over a high heat, stirring with a wooden spoon until quite thick. Cool and add the rest of the Kirsch and the whipped cream.

Cover the peaches with the fig cream and sprinkle the surface with wild strawberries and slivered almonds. Chill and serve.

CHOCOLATE BANANAS

4 Servings

4 bananas
180 gr (6 oz or ¾ cup) sugar
4 teaspoons Kirsch or Cointreau
240 ml (½ pint or 1 cup) double cream

60 grs (2 oz or ½ cup) grated chocolate

Slice bananas in thin rounds into a serving dish. Cook sugar with 2 tablespoons of water and Kirsch to make syrup.

Pour the syrup over the banana slices. Spoon cream on top, sprinkle with chocolate. Chill and serve very cold.

FRUIT SNOW

4 Servings

1 tablespoon lemon juice
4 tablespoon sugar

250 grs (1 lb or 2 cups) fruit pulp
4 eggs whites beaten stiff

Purée of any fruit, cooked or raw, can be used for this quick dessert.

Add lemon juice and sugar to the fruit pulp and fold into stiffly beaten egg whites, adding it a little at a time, to keep the mixture light. Serve in individual dishes with custard (pp. 15 and 187) or cream.

CURRANTS MONT BLANC

6 Servings

1 kg (2 pints or 4 cups) red and white currants
½ kg (1 lb or 2 cups) cottage cheese

250 ml (½ pint or 1 cup) milk
250 grs (8 oz or 1 cup) sugar

Wash and stem the currants and put them in a serving dish.

Beat cheese with milk and add sugar, or put through a blender. Mix with the currants and serve very cold.

WHIPPED AVOCADO

6 Servings

3 avocados

240 grs (8 oz or 1 cup) sugar

4 tablespoons fresh lemon juice

2–3 tablespoons Creme de Menthe liqueur

1 lemon cut in wedges

Cut avocados, remove pulp, taking care not to damage skin as these will be used as shells for serving. Mash the pulp, or better still, put through a blender, with sugar, lemon juice and liqueur, until the mixture is creamy. Pile into shells and chill. Serve garnished with wedges of lemon.

Fruit Desserts to be Served Hot or Cold

BARNABY'S BAKED APPLE SLICES

4–6 Servings

4 large apples
butter
juice and zest of 1 lemon

3 tablespoons honey
4 tablespoons sesame seeds
$\frac{1}{4}$ teaspoon ground cinnamon

Wash and core the apples. Leave the peel on – it adds flavour. Slice the apples and arrange half of them in a buttered ovenproof dish. Spoon over half the lemon juice mixed with the honey, sesame seeds, finely chopped lemon zest and cinnamon. Repeat with remaining ingredients. Bake in the oven at 175°C (350°F or Gas Mark 3) for 30 minutes. Serve hot or cold, topped with whipped cream or sour cream.

DIFFERENT PRUNES

6 Servings

360 grs (12 oz or 1½ cups) stoned
and sieved prunes
1 tablespoon lemon juice
$\frac{1}{4}$ crushed cumin seeds (or fennel,
or caraway)

4 egg whites
pinch salt
60 grs (2 oz or 4 tablespoons)
castor sugar

Blend sieved prunes, lemon juice and cumin seeds.

Beat egg whites into stiff peaks, gradually incorporate salt and sugar, gently fold into the prune purée. Pour into a buttered 1½ litre (3 pint or 6 cup) oven dish and stand in a shallow pan of hot water. Bake in the oven pre-heated to 175°C (350°F or Gas Mark 3) for 45 to 55 minutes.

Serve hot or cold.

SCANDINAVIAN PRUNE DESSERT

6 Servings

½ kg (1 lb or 4 cups) cooked prunes
90 grs (3 oz or ½ cup) whole
blanched almonds
3 eggs

120 grs (4 oz or ½ cup) sugar
¼ litre (½ pint or 1 cup) milk
¼ litre (½ pint or 1 cup) whipped
cream

Pit the prunes and insert an almond into each. Put in an oven-proof dish.

Separate eggs, beat yolks with sugar until light. Gently heat milk, remove from heat as soon as it reaches boiling point and stir into yolks. Leave this custard mixture to cool. Pre-heat oven to 175°C (350° For Gas Mark 3). Beat egg whites into a stiff foam, fold into the custard, pour over prunes and bake for 40 minutes. Serve hot or cold, with whipped cream.

RHODE ISLAND RHUBARB BROWN BETTY

6 Servings

375 grs (12 oz or 3 cups) cut
rhubarb
butter
180 grs (6 oz or 2 cups) stale cake
crumbs

juice of one orange
120 grs (4 oz or ½ cup) sugar

Wash rhubarb, put in a bowl, pour boiling water over it to cover, leave to stand for 10 minutes then drain. This reduces the excess sourness. Put rhubarb in a buttered oven dish and cover with cake crumbs. Pour on the orange juice and sprinkle top with sugar. Bake in the oven pre-heated to 175°C (350°F or Gas Mark 3) for 30 to 40 minutes.

Serve hot or cold.

Mousses

LEMON MOUSSE

4 Servings

5 egg yolks	5 egg whites, beaten stiff
180 grs (6 oz or ¾ cup) sugar	redcurrant jelly (p. 214)
juice of 2 lemons	

Beat the egg yolks with sugar until light and lemon-coloured. Add lemon juice and mix well. Stir over hot water in the top of a double boiler until thick. Remove from heat and fold in egg whites. Pour into a serving dish and chill in the refrigerator. Decorate with redcurrant jelly.

COLOMBIAN BLACK COFFEE MOUSSE

6 Servings

15 grs (½ oz or 2 tablespoons) gelatine	240 grs (8 oz or 1 cup) sugar
	water
480 ml (1 scant pint or 2 cups) strong black coffee	2 egg whites
	whipped cream

Dissolve gelatine in the hot black coffee. Moisten the sugar with just enough water to be absorbed without going runny and simmer the sugar in a heavy based saucepan until it is a very light syrup (p. 217). Remove from heat, cool slightly. Pour the coffee into the syrup and stir well. Chill until almost set. Beat the egg whites to stiff peaks and fold into the mixture. Chill. Serve with sweetened whipped cream.

STRAWBERRY MOUSSE

8 Servings

360 grs (12 oz or 2¼ cups) strawberries	¼ litre (½ pint or 1 cup) double cream
1 teaspoon lemon juice	120 grs (4 oz or ½ cup) sugar
⅛ teaspoon salt	2 egg whites, beaten stiff

63

Hull the strawberries, wash in cold water if necessary. Drain well.

Force the strawberries through a strainer and mix the purée with the lemon juice and a small pinch of salt. Whip cream, beat gently into the strawberry purée with a whisk and add the sugar. Fold in egg whites, pour into a serving bowl and chill.

CHOCOLATE MOUSSE

4 Servings

120 grs (4 oz or ⅔ cup) bitter chocolate in pieces	4 tablespoons double cream
60 grs (2 oz or 4 tablespoons) sugar	4 egg yolks, slightly beaten
	4 stiffly beaten egg whites

Melt the chocolate in a double saucepan, stirring to a smooth paste with a wooden spoon. Remove from heat and add sugar, cream and egg yolks. Stir thoroughly. Fold in the stiffly beaten egg whites, lifting the mixture high during the folding. Pour into individual dessert glasses. Chill several hours in refrigerator.

GRAPEFRUIT MOUSSE

4 Servings

5 raw yolks	2 tablespoons lemon juice
180 grs (6 oz or ¾ cup) sugar	5 egg whites
juice of 1 grapefruit	

Beat yolks with sugar until light and pale. Transfer to a double boiler add fruit juice and heat over simmering water until the mixture becomes thick and creamy, stirring all the time.

Remove from heat and allow to cool.

Beat egg whites until very stiff, fold into the grapefruit mixture, pour into a serving dish and chill.

ZABAIONE (Hot)

Zabaione, or zabaglione, a creamy mousse, is served as a dessert on its own and as a sauce for other desserts. It is a most rewarding preparation to make and only overcooking can ruin it.

4 Servings

210 gr (7 oz or 1 cup) castor sugar	2 dcl (2 gills or 1 cup) Marsala
6 egg yolks	flavouring

Beat sugar and yolks until the mixture turns light and begins to form a ribbon. Add Marsala and, whisking all the time, heat in a double boiler over very low heat until the zabaione becomes frothy and stiff, but *do not allow to boil*, or your zabaione will curdle. Whisk in flavouring of your choice (vanilla, orange or lemon sugar, chocolate, Kirsch, Kummel, Maraschino, Grand Marnier, etc.), and serve at once in warmed goblets. Dry white wine, Madeira, Port, Sherry or Champagne can be used instead of Marsala.

ZABAIONE (Cold)

Prepare as above, flavour to taste and, as soon as the sauce acquires its characteristic velvety and frothy consistency, remove from heat, decant into a chilled bowl whisking all the time. When the zabaione cools down, whisk into 1 dcl (1 gill or ½ cup) whipped cream and keep in refrigerator, but do not freeze. It will remain unimpaired for several days. Delicious with fresh soft fruit.

Rice Desserts

DESSERT RICE

Rice forms the basis of many exquisite sweet dishes. Dessert rice can be made into borders, to be filled with fruit, sweet croquettes and various puddings.

6 Servings

1 litre (2 pints or 4 cups) milk
flavouring: vanilla pod, lemon or
    orange peel, rose water, or
    orange blossom water
125 grs (4 oz or 9 tablespoons) rice
75 grs (2½ oz or 5 tablespoons)
    sugar

30 grs (1 oz or 2 tablespoons)
    butter
¼ teaspoon salt
4 raw yolks

Bring the milk gently to the boil with the flavouring of your choice. Remove from heat and leave.

Wash the rice, bring to the boil in water, drain at once, rinse and drain thoroughly again.

Strain the milk, add the rice to it with the sugar, butter and salt. Stir gently, bring to the boil, then cover and simmer on lowest possible heat either on the top of the stove or, better still, in the oven, for half an hour, without disturbing the rice. Remove from heat, taste, add more sugar if necessary, carefully stir in yolks and use for hot rice desserts.

For cold rice desserts, cook as above and when done stir in 1 dcl (1 gill or ½ cup) fresh cream.

RICE FLANS

1 flan case baked 'blind' (pie
    shell) (p. 185)
2–3 tablespoons chopped crystal-
    lised fruit

dessert rice (see above)
sugar
1–2 tablespoons Kirsch

Fill the flan case with dessert rice mixed with crystallised fruit, sprinkled with Kirsch, or other liqueur. Do not fill right to the top, but leave an edge 3½ mm (⅛ inch). Sprinkle with sugar and bake in a moderate oven 190°C (375°F or Gas Mark 4) for 25–30 minutes.

There are innumerable variations on this theme. You can fill the flan case ¾ full of dessert rice, top with halved fresh peaches or apricots dipped in Kirsch and sprinkled with sugar, or with sliced pineapple, or apples, or quartered pears, sliced bananas, dipped in rum and sprinkled with brown sugar, cooked or preserved plums, cherries, etc.

MERINGUED RICE FLAN

Prepare rice flan as described (see above) using dessert rice mixed with crystallised or fresh diced fruit, sprinkled with Kirsch and sugar. Cover with meringue, sprinkle with fine sugar and bake in a very hot oven to set and colour the meringue lightly.

RICE GATEAU

Cook dessert rice as described. Coat a charlotte mould with caramel, i.e. heat the mould with a few tablespoons of sugar moistened with a little water, until sugar becomes brown. Rotate the mould so that its inside becomes evenly coated with the caramelised sugar.

Fill the mould with dessert rice, put in a bain-marie (a shallow pan of hot water) and bake in a moderate oven for 25–30 minutes.

This Rice Gâteau can be served either hot or cold.

RICE À L'IMPÉRATRICE

125 grs (4 oz or ½ cup) vanilla-flavoured dessert rice (p. 66)
3 tablespoons chopped crystallised fruit
1–2 tablespoons Kirsch or other liqueur

2 dcl (½ pint or 1 cup) custard (p. 15)
gooseberry jelly
2 dcl (2 gills or 1 cup) whipped cream

Cook the rice as described and allow to cool.

Soak the fruit in Kirsch and mix with rice. Stir in custard. Spread gooseberry jelly in a 1¼ cm (½ inch) layer on the bottom of a charlotte mould. Fold whipped cream into rice, spoon the mixture into the mould and chill.

Turn out on to a chilled dish before serving.

BAKED RICE PUDDING

90 grs (3 oz or 6 tablespoons) rice, washed and drained
30 grs (1 oz or 2 tablespoons) butter

90 grs (3 oz or 6 tablespoons) sugar
1 litre (2 pints or 4 cups) creamy milk
nutmeg

Butter a pie dish, put in rice, butter, sugar and milk. Sprinkle with grated nutmeg and put in the lower part of a slow oven 149°C (300°F or Gas Mark 2) for 30 minutes. Stir and continue to bake for another 15–20 minutes. Stir again and then leave undisturbed for 2 hours.

The above is the classical English recipe for rice pudding, but it can be varied in many ways. You can flavour it with lemon rind instead of nutmeg, slip a fresh bay leaf into it, add raisins and almonds to it, beat in an egg or two, enrich it with cream, colour it with grated chocolate or strawberry jam. You can pour caramelised sugar on it and glaze the top or cover it with meringue and bake it in the oven, as described in the recipe for Meringued Rice Flan (p. 67).

ORIENTAL RICE CAKE

125 grs (4 oz or 1 cup) self-raising flour
pinch baking powder
90 grs (3 oz or 6 tablespoons) butter
60 grs (2 oz or 6 tablespoons) sultanas
30 grs (1 oz or 2 tablespoons) currants

60 grs (2 oz or 6 tablespoons) seedless raisins
1 tablespoon grated lemon rind
125 grs (4 oz or 1 cup) ground rice
small pinch salt
2 well whisked eggs
1 dcl (1 gill or ½ cup) milk
90 grs (3 oz or 6 tablespoons) soft brown sugar

Sift flour with baking powder into a bowl. Cut butter into small pieces and rub it into the flour. Add sultanas, currants, raisins, lemon rind and rice. Season with a little salt. Stir well. Beat the

68

eggs into the milk, then stir the mixture into the rice and flour. Add sugar, mix thoroughly, put into a lightly greased tin and bake in a very moderate oven 177°C (350°F or Gas Mark 3) for 1¼ hours. Test for readiness : insert a knife in the centre of the cake – if it comes out dry, the cake is baked. If not, continue for another 15–20 minutes, testing again after 10 minutes.

RICE GATEAU WITH CARAMEL

Prepare Dessert Rice (p. 66) and flavour with vanilla and lemon sugar. Put into a charlotte mould lined with caramelised sugar (p. 221) set in a pan of water, and bake in a moderate oven 190°C (375°F or Gas Mark 4) for about 30 minutes. Serve with caramel syrup or caramel flavoured custard (p. 15 or 217).

JAPANESE RICE CUTLETS WITH SULTANA SAUCE

6–8 Servings
3 cups cooked rice	breadcrumbs
1 egg	oil for deep frying
1 tablespoon brown sugar	

Stir the egg and sugar into the cold rice. Shape into small round patties. Roll in breadcrumbs and deep fry in hot oil until golden brown. Serve hot with Sultana sauce (p. 194).

KHIR / INDIAN MILK PUDDING

6 Servings
90 grs (3 oz or 6 tablespoons) rice	90 grs (3 oz or 1 cup) ground almonds
½ litre (1 pint or 2 cups) milk	
2½ tablespoons sugar	3–4 tablespoons flaked coconut
¼ teaspoon salt	½ teaspoon orange blossom water
¼ teaspoon ground cinnamon	3 tablespoons crystallised fruit
45 grs (1½ oz or 4 tablespoons) pistachio nuts	coconut cream (p. 218)
	Gula Malacca syrup (p. 48)

Put rice with milk, sugar, salt and cinnamon to cook over medium heat for 7–8 minutes. Chop pistachio nuts and add them with almonds, coconut, orange blossom water and crystallised fruit to the rice mixture. Stir, cover and continue to cook until the rice is done. Serve chilled, with coconut cream and syrup as for Gula Malacca. If coconut cream is not available, serve sweetened whipped cream.

PEARS A L'IMPERATRICE

4 Servings

210 grs (7 oz or 1 cup) rice
360 ml (¾ pint or 1½ cups) milk
pinch of salt
1 vanilla bean
360 grs (12 oz or 1½ cups) sugar

2 egg yolks
1½ dcl (¼ pint or ½ cup) double
cream
4 large pears
juice of 1 lemon

Boil the rice for 2 minutes in water.

Boil the milk with salt and a vanilla bean. Strain.

Drain the rice and add milk. Reduce heat and simmer for 15 minutes. Remove from heat and stir in half the sugar and the egg yolks. Mix carefully. Cool. Whip cream and stir into rice carefully.

Make a syrup by boiling remaining sugar with 240 ml (½ pint or 1 cup) water. Reduce heat and simmer the pears whole or in halves until tender.

Put the rice mixture in a serving dish and arrange the pears on top. Add lemon juice to syrup and pour over pears.

LEMON RICE CUSTARD

6 Servings

5 tablespoons rice
grated rind of 1 lemon
1 litre (1 quart) milk
30 grs (1 oz or 2 tablespoons)
butter

120 grs (4 oz or ½ cup) sugar
2 beaten eggs
3 tablespoons caramel syrup for
lining (p. 217)

Wash the rice and cook it slowly with lemon rind in milk for one hour. (Be careful not to let the rice stick – if necessary add more milk.) Add butter and sugar, remove from heat and add eggs. Mix well, put into a caramel-lined dish and bake in the oven pre-heated to 175°C (350°F or Gas Mark 3) until the custard sets. Cool and turn out for serving.

Cheese Desserts

FLORENTINE CREAM CHEESE PIE

6 Servings

puff pastry (pp. 181–2)
½ kg (1 lb or 2 cups) cream cheese
180 grs (6 oz or 2 cups) ground almonds
1 tablespoon rose water
120 grs (4 oz or ¾ cup) washed currants

60 grs (2 oz or 4 tablespoons) sugar
1 small packet frozen spinach, cooked, drained and chopped
a little beaten eggs

Line a pie dish with puff pastry, rolled out thin. Mix the rest of ingredients thoroughly, spread in the dish, cover with strips of pastry, brush the top with beaten egg and bake in the oven 190°C (375°F or Gas Mark 4) for ½ hour.

SWISS CREAM CHEESE AND BLACK CHERRY FLAN (PIE)

4 Servings

1 flan case, baked 'blind' (p. 185)
240 grs (8 oz or 1 cup) cream cheese
1 egg
90 grs (3 oz or 6 tablespoons) sugar

½ teaspoon vanilla essence
240 grs (8 oz or 1¼ cups) stoned black cherries

Blend all ingredients, except cherries, until smooth and creamy. Arrange cherries in the flan case, pour the cheese mixture over them and chill until ready to serve.

PASKHA TRADITIONAL RUSSIAN EASTER SWEET

8–10 Servings

1 kg (2 lb or 4 cups) well drained, unsalted cream cheese
⅛ teaspoon salt
60 grs (2 oz or 6 tablespoons) seedless raisins
60 grs (2 oz or 6 tablespoons) mixed candied fruits
60 grs (2 oz or ⅔ cup) shopped blanched almonds

120 grs (4 oz or ½ cup) unsalted butter
240 grs (8 oz or 1 cup) sugar
5 egg yolks
1 beaten egg
2½ dcl (½ pint or 1 cup) whipped cream
1 teaspoon vanilla essence

Rub the cheese through a fine sieve, add salt, raisins, candied fruits and almonds. Mix well. Blend butter and sugar, add yolks and beat well. Combine with cheese mixture, add beaten egg, stir, fold in whipped cream.

Heat mixture in a double boiler, over simmering water, stirring constantly until bubbles form around the edge of the pan and mixture thickens enough to coat a spoon. Remove from heat, continue stirring while the mixture cools, add vanilla essence.

The traditional mould for paskha is a pyramid shape, but a clean flowerpot with a hole in the bottom makes a good substitute. Line it with cheesecloth rinsed in water and wrung out, pour the mixture into it, enclose with the cheesecloth and put a small plate or saucer on top with a weight to keep it down. Chill and allow surplus moisture to drain off. Unmould, remove cheesecloth and serve cold.

CREAM CHEESE TARTLETS

sweetened tart pastry (p. 183)

cream cheese filling (p. 189)
butter

Line tart tins with rolled out pastry, fill with cream cheese filling, dot with small pieces of butter and bake in a moderate oven 190°C (375°F or Gas Mark 4) for 25–30 minutes.

HUNGARIAN CREAM CHEESE PANCAKE PIE, WITH MERINGUE (RAKOTT TUROS PALACSINTA

6–8 Servings

240 grs (8 oz or 2 cups) flour
1 teaspoon salt
4 eggs

½ litre (1 pint or 2 cups) milk
cream cheese filling (p. 189)
½ kilo (1 lb or 1 cups) jam

(strawberry, plum, red currant,	3 eggs beaten stiff
etc.)	6 tablespoons icing sugar
2 tablespoons melted butter	castor sugar

Mix flour and salt. Beat eggs with milk, gradually add to flour, whisking to make a smooth batter. Fry pancakes as described (p. 121), browning lightly on both sides. Put pancake on a buttered baking dish, spread with cream cheese filling. Continue in this way until all pancakes are used up, filling with alternate layers of cheese and jam, finishing with a pancake 'lid'. Sprinkle with melted butter, and bake in a very moderate oven 175°C (350°F or Gas Mark 3) for 20 minutes.

Little by little, beat icing sugar into egg whites for a good stiff meringue, spread it over pancakes, return to oven for 7–8 minutes, until the meringue acquires a pale golden colour. Dust with sugar. To serve, cut like a layer cake.

PANCAKE PIE, WITH NUTS

Proceed as above, substituting almond or walnut filling for jam in alternate layers. To make nut filling, combine :

120 grs (4 oz or 1 cup) chopped	1–2 raw egg yolks
almonds (walnuts, hazel or	3 tablespoons sugar
pecans)	4 tablespoons single cream

Blend well and use as described.

CREAM CHEESE AND APRICOT FLAN

6 Servings

20 cm (8 inch) flan case, baked	in syrup and well-drained (or
'blind' (p. 185)	1 small tin apricot halves)
240 grs (8 oz or 1 cup) cream	2 tablespoons red currant jelly
cheese	2 teaspoons water
120 grs (4 oz or ½ cup) sugar	1 tablespoon lemon juice
1 dozen apricots, halved, poached	angelica to decorate

Blend cheese and sugar, spread evenly over the bottom of the flan case. Arrange the apricots on top, cut side down. Put the red-currant jelly, water and lemon juice into a small pan, stir over a low heat to dissolve, boil fast to thicken and make more syrupy and spoon over the fruit. Decorate with angelica cut in fancy shapes. Serve cold.

BASIC CHEESE CAKE

3 tablespoons butter
60 grs (12 oz or 1 cup) wholewheat biscuit crumbs
4 yolks
180 grs (6 oz or ¾ cup) sugar
480 grs (1 lb or 2 cups) cottage
  cheese

1 tablespoon flour
1 tablespoon semolina
120 ml (4 oz or ½ cup) sour cream
grated rind of 1 lemon
2 tablespoons chopped peel, or
  white raisins (optional)
4 egg whites

Butter a hinged flan (pie) tin. Mix biscuit crumbs with butter
and use to line the tin, pressing down to make an even, well-
packed crust. Pre-heat oven to 190°C (375°F or Gas Mark 4).
Beat yolks with sugar until light and creamy. Rub cheese through
a sieve, add the yolks with all the rest of the ingredients, except egg
whites. Mix thoroughly. Beat egg whites until very stiff, fold into
the cheese mixture, put into the prepared flan tin and bake for
40–45 minutes. Turn off heat and leave the cake in the oven for
15–20 minutes before taking it out.

MELOPITA

Cheese cake recipe from Ancient Greece

Pastry:
180 grs (6 oz or 1½ cups) sifted
  flour
pinch salt

120 grs (4 oz or ½ cup) lard
1 egg
4 tablespoons sesame seeds

Filling:
750 grs (1½ lb or 3 cups) sieved
  cottage cheese
pinch salt
180 grs (6 oz or ½ cup) honey

¼ teaspoon ground cinnamon (or
  ⅛ teaspoon ground cloves)
5 eggs
2 tablespoons toasted sesame seeds

Pre-heat oven to 235°C (450°F or Gas Mark 7).

Cut the lard into the flour and salt. Add egg and sesame seeds.
Pat into a 22 cm (9 inch) pie tin. Bake in the oven for 10 minutes,
or until crust begins to turn golden.

Add honey, salt and spice to cheese, blend well. Add eggs, one
at a time, beating each time. Pour into pie crust. Sprinkle top with
sesame seeds. Put back in the oven. Reduce heat to 175°C (350°F
or Gas Mark 3). Bake for 45 minutes or until a knife inserted in
the centre comes out clean.

FLORIDA BLUEBERRY CHEESECAKE

10 Servings

½ kg (1 lb or 2 cups) softened
  cream cheese
4 beaten egg yolks
4 tablespoons lemon juice
grated rind of ½ lemon
2 tablespoons gelatine
1 dcl (1 gill or ½ cup) cold water
4 egg whites

sugar
½ dcl (½ gill or ⅓ cup) double
  cream
90 grs (3 oz or 1½ cups) cracker
  (biscuit) crumbs
butter
250 grs (½ lb or 1½ cups) blueberries

Combine cream cheese with yolks, lemon juice and rind and beat the mixture until smooth. Soften gelatine in cold water, dissolve it in the top of a double boiler over simmering water and add to the cheese mixture. Beat whites until they are stiff and little by little add 4 tablespoons sugar. Whip cream. Gradually fold into the cheese mixture alternate spoonfuls of meringue and whipped cream.

Mix cracker crumbs with 120 grs (4 oz or ½ cup) sugar and 120 grs (4 oz or ½ cup) butter. Press the mixture firmly against the bottom and sides of a well-buttered flan tin. Bake in a hot oven 204°C (400°F or Gas Mark 5) for 10 minutes, remove and allow shell to cool. Arrange a layer of fresh blueberries, washed and well drained, on the bottom of the flan case and add the cheesecake mixture. Chill and serve.

This cheesecake is equally delicious with any other soft fruit.

MITHA DAHI

This is a simple and delicious Indian sweet.

4–6 Servings

½ kg (1 lb or 2 cups) cottage
  cheese
pinch saffron
2 tablespoons milk

½ kg (1 lb or 2 cups) icing sugar
4–5 ground cardamom seeds
grated nutmeg

Make sure the cheese is well drained. Steep saffron in milk for half an hour.

Mix cheese with saffron-flavoured milk, sugar and cardamom. Rub the mixture through a sieve or pass through a blender. Transfer to a serving dish, sprinkle the top with nutmeg and serve chilled.

CANADIAN PINEAPPLE CHEESECAKE

23 cm (9 inch) spring form pan is recommended
480 gr (1 lb or 2 cups) cream cheese
480 gr (1 lb or 2 cups) cottage cheese
6 eggs

210 gr (7 oz or 1½ cups) sifted icing sugar
1 small tin (80 gr or 6 oz) evaporated milk
1½ teaspoons lemon juice
2 tablespoons flour
½ teaspoon salt
13–14 Graham wafers

for topping:
1 tin crushed pineapple
2 tablespoons cornstarch

3 tablespoons icing sugar

Beat cheeses together. One by one, add eggs, then sugar, milk, lemon juice, flour and salt, ensuring that each ingredient is well blended in before adding the next. Pre-heat oven to 150°C (300°F or Gas Mark 2).

Using Graham wafers make crust according to directions on box. Line pan with graham wafer mixture. Pour in cheese mixture. Bake in the oven for about 2 hours until top is golden brown and firm. *Allow to cool with oven door open.* Refrigerate.

Drain the pineapple. Using 240 ml (8 oz or 1 cup) of the juice, bring it to the boil with sugar. Cook until sugar dissolves. Blend cornflour with 2–3 tablespoons pineapple juice, blend into syrup and continue to cook, stirring constantly, until the syrup thickens. Add drained crushed pineapple. Remove from heat, cool and put on cold cheese cake.

CHEESECAKE requiring no Cooking

60 gr (2 oz or 1 cup) wholewheat biscuit crumbs
2 tablespoons melted butter
sugar
½ teaspoon cinnamon
1 small fresh or tinned crushed pineapple
pinch salt
3 lightly beaten egg yolks

2 tablespoons gelatine
4 tablespoons cold water
½ kilo (1 lb or 2 cups) cream cheese
1 teaspoon lemon rind
2 tablespoons lemon juice
3 stiffly beaten egg whites
2½ dcl (½ pint or 1 cup) whipped cream

Mix biscuit crumbs with butter, 1 tablespoon sugar and cinnamon and use mixture to line a hinged flan tin. Drain pineapple and keep the juice. In a double boiler, mix 120 gr (4 oz or 8 tablespoons) sugar, salt, 1 dcl (1 gill or ½ cup) pineapple juice, yolks, and cook over boiling water until smooth and thickened, stirring constantly. Soak gelatine in cold water for 5 minutes, add to mixture in double boiler and stir until dissolved, then chill the mixture until it begins to set. Add pineapple, cheese and lemon rind and juice. Fold in egg whites and whipped cream. Pour into flan tin, smooth the top, chill for 10–12 hours and serve.

CHEESE STRUDEL

Strudel dough (pp. 183–4)
melted butter
120 gr (4 oz or ½ cup) sugar
60 gr (2 oz or ½ cup) fine breadcrumbs
pinch cinnamon
90 gr (3 oz or 9 tablespoons)
  raisins

2 tablespoons butter
6 egg yolks
½ kilo (1 lb or 2 cups) well
  drained cream cheese
¼ litre (½ pint or 1 cup) sour
  cream
6 egg whites, beaten stiff

Brush stretched strudel dough with melted butter, sprinkle with 4 tablespoons sugar, breadcrumbs, cinnamon and raisins. Blend butter with egg yolks, add cheese and mix well. Add sour cream, the rest of the sugar, and stir. Fold in egg whites and spread the mixture over strudel. Roll up, put on a greased baking sheet and bake in a moderately hot oven, 205°C (400°F or Gas Mark 5) for 20 minutes, then lower to 175°C (350°F or Gas Mark 3) and bake for 35–40 minutes, brushing with melted butter a couple of times during baking.

Other suggestions for strudel fillings :
1. Sliced apples and chopped walnuts or almonds
2. Almonds blended with egg yolks and sugar
3. Mixed dried fruit and shredded coconut
4. Turkish delight (p. 201), chopped, mixed with raisins and walnuts and flavoured with nutmeg
5. Buttered breadcrumbs, hazelnuts and stoned cherries or brandied morello cherries

Cakes and Gâteaux

SPONGE CAKE

This is a delicate sponge cake. It is important to bake it in a very moderate oven. If the oven is too hot, the cake will fail to rise properly and will be heavy; or it will rise too quickly and collapse. If the oven is not hot enough, you may have a lump forming on the bottom. This cake can be filled and covered with a cream icing (p. 191), or lightly dusted with icing sugar. It makes an excellent basis for trifles and other desserts.

120 grs (4 oz or 1 cup and 2 tablespoons) sifted cake flour
small pinch salt
6 raw yolks
grated rind and juice of 1 lemon

180 grs (6 oz or ¾ cup) castor sugar
6–7 whites of egg
½ teaspoon cream of tartar

Pre-heat oven to 175°C (350°F or Gas Mark 3).

Sift the flour with salt twice and leave in a sifter. Beat yolks until thick, gradually beat in lemon rind and juice. Add half the sugar and continue to beat thoroughly until egg and sugar are completely amalgamated and the mixture is light and fluffy. Fold in flour, sifting it in little by little.

Whisk egg whites with cream of tartar and, as they begin to stiffen, little by little incorporate the remaining sugar, beating all the time. Fold the whites into the yolk mixture very gently, lifting it delicately.

Pour the batter into an ungreased pan, a tub pan if you have one for preference. Bake for 50–60 minutes. Invert the pan over a wire cake rack and leave to cool completely before removing the pan.

79

PARIS-BREST

This is a great Parisian speciality, which is not difficult to make and tastes and looks most rewarding.

6 Servings
chou paste (p. 182)
chopped almonds

almond cream (p. 187) or crème praline (p. 218) or crème chantilly (p. 189)

Proceed to prepare chou paste exactly as described in recipe for eclairs and leave the paste to cool completely. Using a pastry bag with a wide nozzle, force the paste on to a baking sheet, lined with oiled greaseproof paper, in the shape of a ring. Sprinkle generously with chopped almonds – the top should really be well encrusted with them. Bake for 40–45 minutes in the oven pre-heated as for eclairs. Cool on a wire rack, split open, removing the top half of the ring. Using a forcing bag fill liberally with almond cream, (or crème praline, or crème chantilly).

A thick layer of the filling must be visible when the top is replaced. Replace the top and serve.

DEEP SOUTH DEVIL'S FOOD CAKE

6–8 Servings
2 tablespoons butter
$\frac{1}{2}$ kg (1 lb or 2 cups) sugar
4 raw yolks
$\frac{1}{4}$ litre ($\frac{1}{2}$ pint or 1 cup) sour cream

180 grs (6 oz or 1 cup pieces) plain chocolate
180 ml (6 oz or $\frac{3}{4}$ cup) water
300 grs (10 oz or $2\frac{1}{2}$ cups) sifted flour
4 egg whites

Cream butter and sugar together. Beat yolks; beat sour. cream into yolks, add butter and sugar and mix well. Melt chocolate in water in top of double boiler and add to the mixture. Add sifted flour to the mixture. Beat the egg whites stiffly and fold into batter. Pour into 2 22 cm (9 inch) buttered baking tins and bake in the oven pre-heated to 175°C (350°F or Gas Mark 3) until a needle inserted in the middle of the cake comes out dry.

When cool and just before serving, add an angelic touch by filling and topping with pure whipped cream (p. 189).

DUTCH APPLE CAKE

6–8 Servings
180 grs (6 oz or $1\frac{1}{2}$ cups) flour
$2\frac{1}{2}$ teaspoons baking powder

4 tablespoons sugar
$\frac{1}{2}$ teaspoon salt

60 grs (2 oz or ¼ cup) butter
120 ml (¼ pint or ½ cup) milk
1 teaspoon vanilla

1 kg (2 lb or 4 cups) sliced cooking apples

For topping:
45 grs (1½ oz or 3 tablespoons) butter
150 grs (5 oz or ⅔ cups) sugar

1 tablespoon flour
1 teaspoon cinnamon
1 tablespoon lemon juice

Sift flour, baking powder, sugar and salt into a bowl. Cut butter into dry ingredients and rub with fingers until it is the consistency or coarse crumbs. Add milk and vanilla and stir until you have a soft dough. Roll dough on a lightly floured board and use it to line a 22 cm (9 inch) flattish ovenproof dish. Press apple slices into dough.

To make topping, cream butter and gradually add the remaining ingredients. Spread on top of apples. Bake in the oven preheated to 250°C (400°F or Gas Mark 5) for 45 minutes. Serve warm with cream.

SAINT-HONORÉ

½ recipe fine lining paste (p. 183)
½ recipe fine chou paste (p. 182)
Cream Saint-Honoré (p. 187)

120 ml (4 oz or ½ cup) double cream

Roll out fine lining paste and make a circle 20 cm (8 inches) in diameter and 1¼ cm (½ inch) thick. Set on a baking sheet, prick in several places with a fork, and moisten the edges with a brush dipped in water. Fill a forcing bag with fine chou paste, and pipe a thin ring of chou paste around the dampened edge of the lining paste circle. Bake in a 205°C (400°F or Gas Mark 5) oven until done (about 30 minutes). Cool on rack.

On a separate baking sheet, pipe 20 or 30 little balls the size of a walnut, brush with beaten egg, and bake in the same oven for about 15 minutes. Cool on rack.

Prepare Cream Saint-Honoré and, at the last moment, whip the cream. Fill the centre of the ring with Cream Saint-Honoré to the top of the chou pastry ring. With a spoon, scoop up the cream into little domes. Pipe a small amount of whipped cream into each little ball and arrange them in a crown, on the ring of chou pastry.

GÂTEAU PITHIVIERS

1 recipe puff pastry (pp. 181–2)   confectioners' sugar
almond cream (pp. 187–8

Roll out the pastry to a thickness of ¾ cm (¼ inch) and cut into 20 cm (8 inch) circle. Collect all leftover pieces, give them two turns, and roll out a second circle of the same diameter but slightly thinner. Put the thinner circle on a moistened metal sheet, press it down gently and prick with a fork in 3 or 4 places. Moisten the edges with a brush dipped in water, and spread with a layer of almond cream 3¼ cm (1¼ inch) thick, leaving about 1¼ cm (½ inch) all round the edges uncovered. Give the second piece of pastry a turn and cover the bottom piece. Press well all around to seal the edges. Pre-heat oven to 220°C (425°F or Gas Mark 6). Brush the top with a thick layer of dissolved powdered sugar and mark the top in the shape of a rosette with the point of a knife. Bake 25–30 minutes, or until done. Serve cold or warm.

CHRISTMAS YULE LOG

This is a symbolic Christmas cake made in the shape of a log. Spread an oblong of warm sponge cake (p. 179) with a thick layer 1¼ cm (½ inch) of chocolate or coffee butter cream (p. 188). Roll into the shape of a log. Decorate with chocolate or coffee butter cream, using a forcing bag with a fluted nozzle, and ice the cake in lengthwise strips to represent the bark of a log.

Sprinkle grated pistachio nuts along the 'bark' and trim with marzipan leaves.

ACCADIAN ANGEL FOOD CAKE

360 ml (12 oz or 1½ cups) egg whites (10–12 egg whites)
1 teaspoon cream of tartar
pinch salt
105 grs (3½ oz or 1 cup) cake flour

360 grs (12 oz or 1½ cups) vanilla castor sugar (p. 113)
1 tablespoon lemon juice
½ tablespoon butter

Whisk egg whites until frothy, add cream of tartar and salt. Beat until stiff but not dry.

Pre-heat oven to 160°C (325°F or Gas Mark 2–2½).

Sift flour and sugar together several times, then fold into egg whites, a small amount at a time. Add lemon juice.

Pour into a buttered 25 cm (10 inch) turk's head baking tin (deep pan with a hole through the middle). Bake for about an hour. Remove from oven and invert the pan on a wire rack. Let stand until cold. Serve with custard (p. 15) or syllabub (p. 45).

VIENNA SACHERTORTE

16 Servings

75 grs (2½ oz or ⅓ cup) butter
240 grs (8 oz or 1 cup) sugar
pinch salt
5 yolks
1 whole egg
240 grs (8 oz or 1⅓ cups) plain or bitter chocolate, in pieces
70 grs (2¼ oz or ¾ cup) ground almonds

5 egg whites
120 grs (4 oz or ¾ cup) apricot jam (p. 213)
½ litre (1 pint or 2 cups) whipped cream (p. 189)
chocolate butter icing (p. 191)
16 blanched almonds

Cream butter, sugar and salt together until light and fluffy. Add the 5 egg yolks and the whole egg and mix well. Melt the chocolate gently, over boiling water, in the top of a double boiler and when melted and smooth, combine with the ground almonds. Add this to the egg mixture and beat well.

Beat the egg whites to stiff peaks and fold into the chocolate mixture. Line three round 20 cm (8 inch) layer baking tins with greaseproof paper and into these evenly pour the mixture. Bake in the oven pre-heated to 175°C (350°F or Gas Mark 3) for 15–20 minutes. Allow to cool for 15 minutes before carefully removing from baking tins. Fold apricot jam into whipped cream and spread between layers of Sachertorte. Ice sides and top of cake with chocolate butter icing.

Decorate with blanched almonds in a pretty pattern. Chill before serving.

GUGELHUPF

8–10 Servings

¼ litre (½ pint or 1 cup) milk
10 grs (⅓ oz or 2 teaspoons) baker's yeast
60 ml (2 oz or ¼ cup) warm water
75 grs (2½ oz or ⅓ cup) butter
120 grs (4 oz or ½ cup) sugar
2 eggs

105 grs (3½ oz or 1 cup) sifted cake flour
60 grs (2 oz or ½ cup) chopped blanched almonds
75 grs (2½ oz or ½ cup) chopped candied cherries
2 teaspoons grated lemon zest
icing sugar

Scald milk and let cool. Sprinkle yeast over warm water, stir until dissolved and add to milk. Cream butter with sugar. Add eggs one at a time, beating after each addition. Add flour alternately with yeast mixture, blending well. Stir in chopped almonds, cherries and grated lemon zest.

Pour into a 3 pint Turk's Head baking mould, cover and put in a warm place to rise for about 2 hours. Bake in the oven preheated to 190°C (375°F or Gas Mark 4) for 35 minutes. Cool on a wire rack and remove from mould. Sprinkle with icing sugar.

STRAWBERRY SHORTCAKE

6 Servings

1 kg (2 lb or 6 cups) fresh strawberries	2 tablespoons baking powder
	pinch salt
270 grs (9 oz or 1 cup and 2 tablespoons) sugar	90 grs (3 oz or 6 tablespoons) butter
225 grs (7½ oz or 2 cups) cake flour	150 ml (5 oz or ⅔ cup) milk
	whipped cream (p. 189)

Before preparing base for shortcake, if necessary wash and dry the strawberries carefully. Hull them, bruise slightly, cover with 240 grs (8 oz or 1 cup) sugar and let stand.

Sift flour, remaining sugar, baking powder and salt into a bowl. Cut in butter until the mixture looks like fine crumbs. Add milk and stir until you have a soft dough. Knead gently on a lightly floured board. Pat half the dough into a well buttered 20 cms (8 inch) round cake tin. Dot with butter and spread remaining dough on top. Bake in the oven pre-heated to 235°C (450°F or Gas Mark 7) for 10–15 minutes. Separate layers and cool.

Heap sweetened strawberries between layers and on top of cake.

Serve with whipped cream, or for special occasions, pipe whipped cream all over it and decorate with a few perfect strawberries.

Variations: Raspberry shortcake is made as above and is delicious.

For peach shortcake, use fresh, peeled and sliced ripe peaches.

KENTISH COB NUT CAKE

6–8 Servings

240 grs (8 oz or 1 cup) butter	6 stiffly beaten egg whites
½ kg (1 lb or 2 cups) sugar	115 grs (4½ oz or 1½ cups) finely chopped cob nuts (or hazel nuts)
325 grs (11 oz or 3 cups) flour	
pinch salt	praline cream (p. 218)
2½ dcl (½ pint or 1 cup) milk	marzipan leaves (p. 202–3)

Cream butter and sugar together. Sift flour and salt together and little by little add to the butter and sugar, alternating with the milk. Whisk eggs to stiff peaks and gently fold in to the mixture. Then fold in the finely chopped cob nuts. Pour into 22 cm (9 inch) buttered cake tins and bake in the oven pre-heated to 190°C (375°F or Gas Mark 4) for 30 minutes. Cool, fill with praline cream and decorate with marzipan 'cob nuts' and 'leaves'.

BURMESE COCONUT DESSERT CAKE

60 grs (2 oz or ½ cup) flour
150 grs (5 oz or ¾ cup) semolina
1 teaspoon baking powder
pinch salt
120 grs (4 oz or ½ cup) butter
240 grs (8 oz or 1 cup) vanilla
  flavoured sugar (p. 113)
4 eggs yolks

120 grs (4 oz or 1½ cups) grated
  coconut
4 egg whites, beaten stiff
butter for greasing tins

For decoration:
120 ml (¼ pint or ½ cup) cream
¾ tablespoons shredded coconut

Sift flour and semolina, with baking powder and salt. Beat butter and sugar until pale and creamy. Beat in yolks, one by one. Stir in flour mixture. When well mixed, add coconut and blend in.

Lastly fold in egg whites.

Divide mixture in two shallow, greased, 20 cm (8-inch) sandwich tins and bake in a very moderate oven (pre-heated to 177°C – 350°F or Gas Mark 3) for 25 minutes.

Whip the cream, pipe it to decorate the surface of the cake, sprinkle with shredded coconut.

The cake can either be left as two separate cakes dressed in this way, or the whipped cream and shredded coconut can be used for sandwiching it.

Note: If vanilla sugar is not available, allow 1 teaspoon vanilla essence. Coconut cream (p. 218) can be used instead of ordinary cream.

SLIVOVITZ LEMON CAKE WITH GRAPE SAUCE

8 Servings

360 gr (12 oz or 1½ cups) butter
180 gr (6 oz or ¾ cup) caster
  sugar
4 eggs
1 tablespoon lemon juice
120 ml (4 oz or ½ cup) slivovitz
  (plum brandy)

180 gr (6 oz or 1½ cups) flour
1 teaspoon baking powder
90 gr (3 oz or ⅔ cup) icing sugar
pinch cinnamon
¾ teaspoon cornflour
240 gr (8 oz or 1 cup) seedless
  grapes

Pre-heat oven to 180°C (350°F or Gas Mark 3). Grease and lightly flour a 20 cm (8 inch) ring mould.

Stir, all but 2 tablespoons, butter with castor sugar until creamy. Separate eggs, add yolks to butter and sugar and whisk well. Add half the lemon juice and 1½ to 2 tablespoons slivovitz.

Sift flour and baking powder and stir into the butter and sugar mixture.

Beat egg whites until stiff and gradually fold into the dough. Pour the dough into the prepared mould and bake in the oven for 40 minutes. Start testing after 35 minutes, by inserting a wooden cocktail stick. If it comes out clean without any batter sticking to it, the cake is done.

Turn out on to a cooling rack, sprinkle with 2 tablespoons icing sugar and leave to cool completely.

To make the sauce, put the remaining butter, icing sugar, lemon juice, slivovitz and cinnamon into a saucepan. Heat gently and simmer on lowest possible heat for a few minutes just to amalgamate the ingredients. Dilute cornflour with a tablespoon of cold water, blend into sauce, simmer stirring until the sauce thickens. Add grapes, simmer for 30 seconds and remove from heat. To serve cut the cake into portions and spoon the sauce over it.

Small Pastries

MADELEINES

240 grs (8 oz or 1 cup) melted
  butter
240 grs (8 oz or 1 cup) sugar
6 eggs

220 grs (7 oz or 2 cups) sifted
  cake flour
1 teaspoon vanilla sugar (p. 113),
  or lemon, or orange sugar
  (p. 217)

Butter 24 little scallop-shaped tins. Put sugar in a mixing bowl, one by one add eggs, breaking them first into a cup. Beat with a whisk. The mixture will begin to increase in volume and become creamy. Continue to beat until the mixture forms ribbon-like folds. Change to a wooden spoon and, stirring in one direction, gradually work in flour. Add flavoured sugar and lastly stir in melted butter, adding it in a thin trickle. Blend well. Pre-heat oven to 205°C (400°F or Gas Mark 5). Fill scallops half to two-thirds full and bake in the oven for 10–12 minutes, until the madeleines are brown. Remove from tins and cool on a wire rack.

DIAN COHEN'S HAMANTASCHEN

To make 2 dozen:

Filling:
160 grs (5 oz or 1 cup) poppyseeds
60 grs (2 oz or ¼ cup) sugar

90 grs (3 oz or ¼ cup) honey
120 ml (4 oz or ½ cup) milk
1 egg

Dough:
3 eggs
180 grs (6 oz or ¾ cup) sugar
180 ml (6 oz or ¾ cup) oil
juice and grated rind of one

orange
480 grs (1 lb or 4 cups) flour
2 teaspoons baking powder
1 teaspoon salt

To make filling, combine poppyseeds, sugar and honey with milk in a saucepan and cook over a moderate heat, stirring all the time to prevent scorching. Beat egg. Add a little of the hot mixture to egg, then add egg to mixture and cook gently for 2–3 minutes. Leave to cool.

To make dough, combine eggs, sugar and oil. Add orange juice and the grated rind of the orange. Sift flour with baking powder and salt and add gradually to mixture. Let stand for 15 minutes. When easy to handle, roll out on a well floured board. Cut into circles 10 cm (4 inch) in diameter. Put a spoonful of filling in the centre of each pastry circle. Pinch edges of dough together to form a shape like a three cornered hat. Put on a well oiled baking sheet, brush with milk and bake in the oven pre-heated to 190°C (375°F or Gas Mark 4) for 20 minutes, or until nicely brown.

YANKEE DOUGHNUTS

Makes 3 dozen

120 grs (4 oz or ½ cup) butter
180 grs (6 oz or ¾ cup) sugar
3 yolks
120 ml (4 oz or ½ cup) milk
375 grs (12½ oz or 3 cups) flour
½ tablespoon baking powder
⅛ teaspoon salt
1 jigger brandy
3 egg whites
fat or oil for deep frying
icing sugar

Cream butter and sugar together until the mixture is pale. Beat egg yolks into milk and add to butter and sugar. Sift flour, baking powder and salt together and stir well into the butter-sugar and yolk mixture. Add brandy.

Beat the egg whites to stiff peaks and fold into the mixture. On a lightly floured board, pat out the dough. Cut doughnut rings with pastry cutters or different sized glasses. Let stand for 15 minutes before frying. Deep fry in hot fat until brown on one side. Turn and brown the other side. Remove from fat and drain on absorbent kitchen paper. Sprinkle with icing sugar and serve hot or cold.

Doughnuts need not be ring shaped. You can cut out circles or ovals instead of rings. When the doughnuts are cooked, make an incision on one side and fill with whipped cream (p. 189) or jam.

CREAM PUFFS

Proceed in exactly the same way as for making éclairs (p. 89) but place chou paste on a baking sheet in the shape of little balls about 7–8 cm (about 3 inches apart). Brush with beaten egg. Bake as éclairs. Allow to cool. Cut in half and fill with Cream Saint-Honoré (p. 187), or whipped cream (p. 189).

TOASTED CREAM PUFFS

Prepare as cream puffs, brush them with beaten egg, flatten slightly, cover the top with a pinch of chopped almonds, and sprinkle with sugar. Press lightly to make these adhere. Bake, allow to cool, and serve.

CHOCOLATE PROFITEROLLES

½ recipe chou paste (p. 182)
beaten egg
120 ml (¼ pint or ½ cup) con-
    fectioners' custard (p. 187)

250 ml (½ pint or 1 cup)
chocolate sauce (p. 194)

Pipe little balls of chou paste through a forcing bag on to a baking sheet. Brush with beaten egg. Bake in the oven pre-heated to 235°C (450°F or Gas Mark 7) for 15 minutes, then reduce to 175°C (350°F or Gas Mark 3) and bake about 30 minutes longer (until the sides of the profiterolles are rigid). Allow to cool completely. Pierce on the bottom and, using a forcing bag with a small nozzle, fill them with confectioners' custard. Arrange on a serving dish and coat generously with hot chocolate sauce.

ECLAIRS

chou paste (p. 182)
beaten egg

confectioners' custard (p. 187) or
    crème chantilly (p. 189)
fondant icing (p. 191)

prepare chou paste and leave to cool completely. Line baking sheets with oiled greaseproof paper. Pre-heat oven to 235°C (450°F or Gas Mark 7).

Fit a piping bag with a plain round nozzle and fill the bag with cold chou paste. Pipe the paste on to baking sheets in 'fingers' about 8–9 cm (3–3½ inches) long. To ensure uniformity at the ends, cut the paste off with a knife dipped in cold water. Brush éclairs with egg and bake for 30 minutes. Remove and leave on a wire rack to cool.

Split éclairs lengthways without severing completely and, using a forcing bag, fill them with crème chantilly or confectioners' custard, which can be flavoured with vanilla, coffee, chocolate, lemon or orange juice, liqueurs, etc. Ice the top of the éclairs with hot fondant icing flavoured to match the filling.

CREAM CORNETS

Puff Pastry (pp. 181–2)   Crème Patissière (p. 187)
icing sugar

Prepare the puff pastry as described. Roll out to a thickness of $\frac{3}{8}$ cm ($\frac{1}{8}$ inch). Cut into strips about $2\frac{1}{2}$ cm (1 inch) wide and $25\frac{1}{2}$ cm (10 inches) long. Roll these strips around cornet-shaped moulds. Put the cornets on a moistened baking sheet, and let them rest for 10 minutes. Brush with egg, and bake in a hot oven 225°C (425°F or Gas Mark 6) for 12 to 15 minutes.

Sprinkle cornets with icing sugar and put in the oven to glaze. As soon as they glisten, take them out. Leave until quite cold.

Using a forcing bag with a round nozzle or a cornet of grease-proof paper, fill the cornet with crème patissière. Or you can fill the cornet with chantilly – sweetened whipped cream (p. 189).

BABA AU RHUM

6 Servings
Dough:

60 grs (2 oz or 4 tablespoons)   15 grs ($\frac{1}{2}$ oz or 1 cake) fresh yeast
   butter   120 grs (4 oz or 1 cup) flour
4 tablespoons seedless raisins   4 tablespoons sugar
1 tablespoon rum $\frac{1}{8}$ teaspoons salt
90 ml (3 oz or 6 tablespoons) milk   2 beaten eggs

Syrup: 120 ml (4 oz or $\frac{1}{2}$ cup) rum
$\frac{1}{2}$ kg (1 lb or 2 cups) sugar   2 tablespoons lemon juice
360 ml (12 oz or $1\frac{1}{2}$ cups) water   crème chantilly (p. 189)

Take butter out of refrigerator to soften it at room temperature. Leave raisins to soak in rum.

Scald milk, remove from heat leave until lukewarm. Break up yeast, add to milk, stir and leave to stand for 10 minutes.

Warm your mixing bowl. Put in flour and stir in yeast and milk mixture. Add sugar, salt and eggs. Beat well, cover with a clean cloth and leave for an hour in a warm place to rise.

Add butter, beat it in energetically and continue to work the dough until it stops sticking to your hands and becomes soft and glistening. Add raisins and mix well.

Put the dough into a large, or smaller individual, well-buttered moulds with a hole in the middle, (in France special fluted 'Turk's head' moulds are used), filling them only up to one-third of their height. Cover with greaseproof paper and leave in a warm place, away from draughts for 1½–2 hours, or until it rises to the top of the moulds.

Bake in the oven pre-heated to 220°C (425°F or Gas Mark 6) for 13–15 minutes. Allow to cool before turning out of the moulds into a serving bowl. Slowly bring sugar and water to the boil, simmer for 5 minutes, add rum and lemon juice, cook gently for a further 2 minutes and remove from heat.

Pour hot, but not boiling, syrup over babas, spooning it over at intervals until babas imbibe all the syrup. Leave until quite cold. Fill the centres of babas with crème chantilly, or serve it separately.

BAKLAVA

This is a delicious sweet of Greek origin but it is also common to Turkey, Iran, Egypt and other Middle Eastern countries. It is made of filo pastry (p. 184), which is similar to stretched strudel dough (p. 183), but must be absolutely tissue-paper thin. It can be bought in Greek shops.

Walnuts, almonds, pistachio nuts and pine kernels, or any combination of these are used in the filling.

In Iran, apricots are used for the syrup and fresh apricots are served with baklava, which is excellent. Our favourite, however, is the classical baklava, with chopped nuts sprinkled between layers of filo, saturated in a syrup made of honey, sugar and lemon juice.

To make 2 dozen baklava pieces :

filo dough (p. 184)   360 grs (12 oz or 1½ cups) unsalted
                                             butter

For filling:
575 grs (1 2oz or 3 cups) chopped   180 grs (6 oz or ¾ cup) sugar
    walnuts

For syrup: 360 ml (12 oz or 1½ cups) water
360 grs (12 oz or 1 cup) honey   juice and rind of 1 lemon
360 grs (12 oz or 1½ cups) sugar   2 sticks cinnamon

Have the dough ready, rolled out and stretched into tissue-paper thin sheets.

Gently melt butter. Mix walnuts and sugar for filling. Heat oven to 190°C (375°F or Gas Mark 4). Brush a 20 cm (8 inch) square baking tin with butter, cut filo dough to match. Put one sheet of dough to line the bottom of the tin, brush generously with butter, cover with another sheet of filo, sprinkle with a layer of nut and sugar mixture. Continue in this way, putting in layers of filo, brushing with butter and sprinkling with filling until all is used up. Finish with a sheet of filo on top and tuck in the ends to enclose all the filling. Brush this top layer of dough with plenty of butter. With a sharp knife, score the top into diamond shapes, to determine the size of your baklava pieces. Bake in the oven for 40–45 minutes until golden brown and crisp. To make syrup, boil honey, sugar and water with lemon juice and cinnamon for 5 minutes. Remove lemon rind and cinnamon sticks. Take baking tin out of oven, drain off any surplus fat, pour hot syrup over baklava and leave until cold. Cut into pieces along scored lines, leave in the syrup overnight, or until ready to serve.

Start making syrup about 10 minutes before baklava is baked. It is important to have the syrup freshly made and hot.

Serve as it is, or, for special occasions, with kaymak (p. 220).

EKMEK KADAYIF WITH KAYMAK – Ahmed's and Vikki's recipe

This is a delectable Turkish pastry. Made of the simplest ingredients : stale bread or toast, soaked in water and squeezed dry, lemon juice and honey or sugar and water syrup, it tastes unbelievably good. It is best made out of kadayif – shredded wheat, and must be served with kaymak (p. 220).

Servings
4 shredded wheat biscuits (or stale white bread)
1 litre (1 quart) boiling water
juice of 2 lemons

½ litre (1 pint or 1½ cups) clear honey or syrup made of ½ kg (1 lb or 2 cups) sugar and ½ litre (1 pint or 2 cups) water in which the biscuit or bread is soaked
kaymak (p. 220)

Put shredded wheat biscuits or bread into a bowl, pour boiling water over it and leave to stand for 15–20 minutes. Drain, squeeze out surplus moisture, and line a baking tin with the squeezed out crumbs. Preheat oven to 175°C (350°F or Gas mark 3). Mix lemon juice with honey and pour over bread. Bake for 40–50 minutes, until golden brown. Baste with the lemon and honey syrup from time to time, to impregnate the bread thoroughly.

In the country in Turkey, where an oven may not be available, the ekmek is cooked in a baking tin on top of the cooker, over a low heat, for 25–30 minutes, basting frequently.

Cool, top with kaymak and serve.

PALMIERS

This is a Parisian speciality. Palmiers are delicious and easy to make. Great care should be taken not to burn them during baking, because the sugar in them caramelises very quickly.

Puff pastry (pp. 181–2)   Sugar

Prepare puff pastry. Turn four times. Allow to stand for 15 minutes. Sprinkle board with sugar instead of flour and turn two more times. Roll out to a thickness 3 mm ($\frac{1}{8}$ inch) and cut into a 30 cm (12 inch) square. Fold two sides so that they meet in the centre. Then fold again, making four thicknesses. Allow the strips to settle for a few moments, then cut across in pieces $\frac{3}{4}$ cm ($\frac{1}{4}$ inch) wide.

Put them flat on a baking sheet, at a little distance from each other. Pre-heat oven to 205°C (400°F or Gas Mark 5) and bake until golden. During cooking, the little cakes open into palm leaf shapes.

Meringues

MERINGUE SHELLS

4 stiffly beaten egg whites
240 grs (1 lb or 1 cup) castor
  sugar

1 tablespoon lemon juice
extra castor sugar for dredging

Add sugar to beaten whites a tablespoon at a time, whisking back into a stiff foam after each addition. Beat in lemon juice. Shape with 2 spoons dipped in cold water or, better still, using a forcing bag, pipe into small rounds or ovals on to a baking sheet lined with oiled kitchen paper. Dredge with castor sugar and dry on the lowest shelf of a very slow oven 135°C (275°F or Gas Mark 1) for 1–1¼ hours until the meringues are thoroughly dried and creamy in colour. If you wish to keep the meringues white, reduce heat after 50–60 minutes to 120°F (250°F or Gas Mark ½) and continue to dry very, very slowly. When meringues have to be kept, slow down the drying process. If dried in a gas oven, with the tap set at its lowest and the oven door left ajar, the meringues can be left up to 10–12 hours. This greatly enhances both their crispness and keeping qualities. After taking out of the oven, press the base of each lightly to make a little hollow. Store in an airtight tin.

Meringues can be variously flavoured and tinted with chocolate, coffee, vanilla, fruit juices and purées, etc. They can be filled with sweetened, whipped cream, flavoured to taste, and many other fillings. Here are some examples:

MERINGUE CROQUEMBOUCHE

Small differently coloured and flavoured meringues, built into a pyramid and held together with sugar syrup boiled to crack degree 135°C (275°F) (p. 217).

95

MERINGUE MARIGNAN

Liqueur-flavoured meringues (Kirsch, Maraschino, etc.) decorated with angelica.

MERINGUE ZEPHIRS

Bake small meringues sandwich together with coffee ice cream (p. 166), arrange in a pyramid, chill and serve with Praline sauce (p. 194).

CANADIAN MERINGUES

Small almond-flavoured biscuit-coloured meringues, with a blanched almond trapped in each one.

FONDANT MERINGUES

Prepare very small meringues, sandwich together with whipped cream, flavoured with Maraschino and tinted pink with strawberry purée. Put on their sides, coat lightly with Kirsch-flavoured fondant icing so that the pink filling shows through.

To make Fondant Icing: Mix 120 grs (4 oz or 1 cup) sifted confectioner's sugar with 2 tablespoons milk, flavour with Kirsch or $\frac{1}{4}$ teaspoon almond or vanilla extract and blend until smooth.

SWISS MERINGUES

Small meringues decorated with crystallised fruit and sprinkled with sugar of different colours.

MERINGUE CHANTILLY

Bake meringue as described and sandwich together with sweetened whipped cream (p. 189).

ITALIAN MERINGUE ZEPHIRS

Bake small meringues, sandwich together with rum-flavoured vanilla ice cream, arrange in a pyramid, chill and serve with chocolate-flavoured zabaione (pp. 64–5).

PAVLOVA (Helen Lindqvist's recipe)

There are several variations of these meringue desserts, claimed as traditional both by Australia and New Zealand. The meringue can be flavoured with coffee or chocolate, chopped nuts can be added to it and the finished cake can be filled with any fruit in season.

4 Servings

butter	2 teaspoons vinegar
5 egg whites	½ teaspoon vanilla
⅛ teaspoon salt	whipped cream (p. 189)
240 grs (8 oz or 1 cup) castor sugar	strawberries or passion fruit for decoration

Grease a 25 cm (10 inch) cake tin with butter, but as you are going to bake this cake on top of the tin rather than inside it, you have to butter the outside. Turn the tin upside down, grease the top and sides. This is to allow the meringue to overhang during expansion. Cover the top with a piece of lightly buttered grease-proof paper.

Pre-heat oven to 205°C (400°F or Gas Mark 5).

Beat egg whites with salt until very stiff, gradually beat in sugar, fold in vinegar and vanilla. Pile the mixture on the up-turned tin, put in the oven, close door, turn off the heat at once and leave the meringue to dry off for 1½–2 hours. When done, the meringue will be a deep shell. Peel the paper off the underneath, which now becomes the inside. Turn upside down, fill with whipped cream, decorate with strawberries or sliced passion fruit.

SWISS MERINGUES WITH CHESTNUT PURÉE

meringues (p. 91)	whipped cream (p. 189)
chestnut purée (see Chestnut Pudding (p. 24)	maraschino cherries for garnish

Prepare meringue shells as described. Put into oven pre-heated to 205°C (400°F or Gas Mark 5), turn off heat and leave to dry off in the turned-off oven overnight. Prepare chestnut purée and chill. Just before serving, fill the shells with chestnut purée, top with whipped cream and decorate with cherries.

D

SNOW EGGS

4–6 Servings

4 egg whites
180 grs (6 oz or 12 tablespoons)
  castor sugar
1 litre (2 pints) heated milk

½ kg (1 lb or 2½ cups) fresh sliced
  strawberries (or other fruit)
vanilla custard (p. 15)
1–2 tablespoons toasted, slivered
  almonds

Beat egg whites until they are stiff, gradually adding sugar. Using a wet tablespoon, form the meringue into egg shapes and slip them off into simmering milk. Poach the meringues 2 minutes on each side, turning them once. Remove the eggs with a perforated spoon and dry on kitchen paper. Heap strawberries in a dish, put the eggs on them, pour cold vanilla custard around the eggs, sprinkle with toasted slivered almonds and serve.

CHERRY MERINGUE

4 Servings

1 kg (2 lb) stoned cherries
300 grs (10 oz or 1¼ cups) sugar

2 egg whites

Cook the cherries with 240 grs (8 oz or 1 cup) sugar and 250 ml (½ pint or 1 cup) water. Cook until syrup is thick but make sure cherries keep their shape. Put in a heat-proof serving dish.

Beat the egg whites stiff and add half the remaining sugar gradually, beating until you have a glossy meringue. Spread the meringue over the cherries. Sprinkle with the rest of the sugar and bake at 190°C (375°F or Gas Mark 4) until lightly browned. Serve immediately.

MERINGUED MELON

This luxurious dessert can be made in advance and left until required, as it can be served warm or cold.

4 Servings

2 medium-sized melons
250 grs (8 oz or 1½ cups)
  strawberries
4 peaches

4 tablespoons maraschino
2 egg whites
2 tablespoons sugar

Cut melons in half. Scoop out and discard seeds. Cut the strawberries in half lengthways. Peel and slice peaches. Put strawberries and peaches into melon cups, sprinkle with maraschino or other liqueur and leave in the refrigerator for an hour.

Pre-heat oven to 235°C (450°F or Gas Mark 7). Beat the egg whites until stiff, gradually work in sugar. Top each melon cup with a portion of meringue. Put in the oven just to brown lightly for about 3–4 minutes.

MERINGUES GLACÉES

Fill small meringue shells (p. 95) with spoonfuls of ice cream of your choice. The dessert looks more spectacular if you use several kinds of ice cream. Serve on a napkin covered dish.

Pies, Tarts, Tourtes, Tartlets

PENNSYLVANIA DUTCH SHOOFLY PIE

8 Servings

150 grs (5 oz or 1¼ cups) flour
½ teaspoon baking powder
80 grs (2½ oz or ⅓ cup) sugar
pinch nutmeg
½ teaspoon cinnamon
pinch cloves

90 grs (3 oz or 6 tablespoons)
butter
105 grs (3½ oz or ½ cup) molasses
½ teaspoon soda
¼ litre (½ pint or 1 cup) boiling
hot coffee
short pastry (p. 181)

Combine flour, baking powder, sugar and spices. Cut in the butter and rub in until it is the consistency of rough breadcrumbs. In another bowl, mix the molasses and soda with the boiling hot coffee. Line a 22 cm (9 inch) pie dish with pastry. Pour molasses into pie shell and sprinkle with crumb mixture. Bake in the oven pre-heated to 190°C (375°F or Gas Mark 4) for 40–45 minutes. Serve hot or cold.

SAVANNAH PECAN PIE

4–6 Servings

3 eggs
240 ml (8 oz or 1 cup) sugar
360 grs (12 oz or 1 cup) maple
syrup

120 grs (4 oz or 1 cup) shopped
pecans
122 cm (9 inch) unbaked pie
(tart) shell (p. 76)
halved pecans for decoration

Beat eggs lightly, add sugar, maple syrup, nuts and salt. Pour into unbaked pie shell and bake in the oven pre-heated to 175°C (350°F or Gas Mark 3) for 40 minutes. Decorate with a pattern of halved pecans.

SPICE ISLANDS PIE

8 Servings

3 eggs separated
120 grs (4 oz or cup) butter
240 grs (8 oz or 1 cup) sugar
60 grs (2 oz or ½ cup) coarsely
chopped walnuts
60 grs (2 oz or ½ cup) coarsely
chopped almonds
75 grs (2½ oz or ½ cup) sultanas
75 grs (2½ oz or ½ cup) seedless
raisins

½ teaspoon cinnamon
½ teaspoon cloves
1 teaspoon nutmeg
pinch salt
2 tablespoons cider vinegar
1 uncooked 22 cm (9 inch) pie
(tart) shell (p. 76)
praline cream (p. 218)

Cream egg yolks, butter and half the sugar together. Mix together nuts, dried fruit, spices, salt and vinegar and add to the above. Beat egg whites until stiff and slowly beat remaining sugar into them. Fold into the nut mixture. Pour into pie (tart) shell and bake in the oven pre-heated to 175°C (350°F or Gas Mark 3) for 40 minutes. Serve hot or cold with praline cream.

NEW ZEALAND APPLE AMBER

6 Servings

¼ kg (1 lb) apples
60 grs (2 oz or 4 tablespoons)
sugar
zest of lemon
30 grs (1 oz or 2 tablespoons)
butter

120 ml (4 oz or ½ cup) water
2 eggs separated
short pastry (p. 181)
2 tablespoons castor sugar

Peel and core apples. Stew with sugar, butter, lemon zest and water until tender. Remove from heat, discard the lemon zest. Add egg yolks. Line 22 cm (9 inch) pie dish with pastry and fill with the apple mixture. Bake in the oven pre-heated to 175°C (350°F or Gas Mark 3) until the pastry is golden brown. Whisk the egg whites to stiff peaks, fold in castor sugar and pile on top of apples. Put back in a cool oven until the meringue top is set and slightly golden.

For Apricot and Rhubarb Amber, substitute equivalent amount of apricots or rhubarb for apples.

SPANISH APPLE PIE

6 Servings

6 peeled, cored, baked apples
120 grs (4 oz or ½ cup) sugar
4 beaten eggs

½ litre (1 pint or 2 cups) warm
milk
½ tablespoon butter

Mash the apples and rub them through a sieve. Mix with sugar and eggs. Add milk, stir to blend well, pour into a caramelised pie dish (p. 221), stand it in a pan of hot water and bake until the pie rises and is golden.

TREACLE TART (TRADITIONAL ENGLISH)

6 Servings

90 grs (3 oz or 4 tablespoons) treacle or golden syrup	25 grs ($\frac{3}{4}$ oz or $\frac{1}{2}$ cup) stale white breadcrumbs
grated rind and juice of 1 lemon	short pastry (p. 181)

In a heavy-bottomed pan heat the treacle or golden syrup with lemon rind. Add lemon juice. Remove from heat. Stir in breadcrumbs. Line a 20 cm (8 inch) shallow pie dish with thin rolled out short pastry. Pour in the treacle mixture. Decorate top with a criss-cross pattern of pastry strips and bake in oven pre-heated to 190°C (375°F or Gas Mark 4) for half an hour.

STRAWBERRY TOURTE

Sweet tourtes are a popular dessert in France. They are prepared in the same way as vol-au-vent, often baked 'blind' (p. 185), then filled with frangipane, almond cream, confectioners' custard, jam, cooked or raw fruit, etc.

As with vol-au-vent, you can either replace the lid or leave the tourte open. If the tourte is baked filled, make sure the filling is placed in the middle, without touching the sides, as this would prevent their rising.

6 Servings

Puff pastry (pp. 181–2)	sugar
egg beaten with 1 teaspoon cold water	2 tablespoons Kirsch
1 kg (2 lb or 4 cups) strawberries	120 ml (4 oz or $\frac{1}{2}$ cup) half set red currant jelly (p. 214)

Give the puff pastry 6 turns, cut off a piece and roll out to a thickness of $1\frac{1}{2}$ cm ($\frac{3}{4}$ inch) and line a square baking tin.

Cut 4 bands of pastry $2\frac{1}{2}$ cm (1 inch) wide. Moisten the edges, set the bands of pastry on the edges, press together to join the ends, trimming off two of the bands so that they fit without overlapping, to prevent double thickness at the corners.

Fill the centre with a wad of rolled up paper. Moisten the tops of bands, cover with a lid of rolled-out pastry and seal the edges.

Brush top only with egg. With the point of a knife mark out the lid and score the tops of the side walls at regular intervals.

Pre-heat oven to 235°C (450°F or Gas Mark 7). Put tourte case in the oven and bake for 10 minutes. Reduce oven temperature to 190°C (375°F or Gas Mark 4) and bake until dry and golden. Remove from oven and while still hot carefully cut out the lid, lift it and remove paper.

Sprinkle strawberries with sugar to taste and Kirsch. Fill the tourte case, coat with half-set redcurrant jelly.

CHERRY TOURTE LUCULLUS

Fill baked tourte shell (p. 103) with apple purée, sugared and mixed with one-third its volume of Frangipane Cream (p. 188). Flavour poached cherries with cherry stone liqueur and arrange them in a double circle on top of the apple mixture.

Spoon cherry syrup over the tourte and serve.

OLD ENGLISH MINCE PIES

short or flaky pastry (p. 181)   butter
mincemeat (p. 214)

Line buttered tart cases or individual pie tins with pastry, fill with the mincemeat. Cover with a pastry lid, taking care to prick the top with a fork, to allow steam to escape during baking.

Bake in the oven pre-heated to 235°C (450°F or Gas Mark 7) for 10 minutes. Reduce heat to 175°C (350°F or Gas Mark 3) and bake for further 20 minutes.

Mince pies are traditionally eaten in England between Christmas and Twelfth Night. Originally they were made oblong to represent the manger. They can be cooked in a large tin or in small individual patty tins. Mince pies are good to eat at any time, but only those served during the traditional festive period guarantee fulfilment of a wish made at the first bite.

CARIBBEAN COCONUT CUSTARD PIE

4 Servings
short crust pastry (p. 181)
2½ dcl (½ pint or 1 cup) milk
2 eggs
60 grs (2 oz or ¼ cup) sugar

pinch salt
60 grs (2 oz or ½ cup) freshly
    grated coconut

Roll out the pastry, line a flan ring or pie dish, prick the bottom and keep in refrigerator until ready to use. Heat oven to 205°C (400°F or Gas Mark 5). Bring milk to the boil. Beat eggs lightly with sugar and salt, little by little dilute with milk, stirring all the time. Blend in coconut, pour custard mixture into pastry case, put in the oven. As soon as the pastry browns, reduce heat to 175°C (350°F or Gas Mark 3) continue to bake for 35–40 minutes, until the coconut custard is set.

LEMON MERINGUE PIE

6 Servings

flan case baked 'blind' (p. 185)
30 grs (1 oz or 3 tablespoons) cornflour
2½ dcl (½ pint or 1 cup) water
juice and grated rind of 2 lemons
240 grs (8 oz or 1 cup) sugar

15 grs (½ oz or 1 tablespoon) butter
2 raw egg yolks
2 stiffly beaten egg whites
glacé cherries and angelica for decoration

Mix cornflour with enough water to make a thin cream. Bring the rest of the water to the boil, pour on the cornflour and stir. Return mixture to saucepan, add lemon juice and boil for 5 minutes, stirring constantly. Add half the sugar, butter and grated lemon rind, cool slightly; one by one beat in the yolks and pour the mixture into the flan case.

Gradually whisk sugar into the egg whites, pile on top of the lemon mixture and bake in a slow oven 150°C (300°F or Gas Mark 2) for about ½ hour, until the filling is set and the meringue crisp and a rich creamy colour. Decorate with cherries and angelica and serve cold.

CHOCOLATE MERINGUE PIE

6 Servings

25 cm (10-inch) short pastry pie case, baked 'blind' (p. 185)
2½ dcl (½ pint or 1 cup) milk
vanilla bean
60 grs (2 oz) plain chocolate

1 tablespoon cornflour
2 tbs cold water
120 grs (4 oz or ½ cup) castor sugar
2 raw yolks
2 egg whites

Bake the pastry case and cool. Heat milk gently with vanilla bean and allow to stand for a few minutes to flavour the milk. Remove vanilla bean.

Dissolve chocolate in milk. Mix cornflour with cold water. Heat milk almost to boiling point, stir in cornflour and simmer gently for a couple of minutes, stirring all the time. Add sugar to taste, stir to dissolve, remove from heat and allow to cool slightly.

Add yolks, blend well and pour the mixture into the pie case. Beat egg whites until stiff.

Gradually whisk remaining sugar into egg whites, pile on top of the chocolate mixture and bake in a slow oven 150°C (300°F or Gas Mark 2) for 45 minutes. Serve cold.

YOGOURT LEMON MERINGUE PIE

4 Servings

25 cm (10 inch) pastry case, baked blind (p. 185)
180 grs (6 oz or ¾ cup) sugar
3 level tablespoons cornflour
120 ml (¼ pint or ½ cup) lemon juice

1 teaspoon grated lemon rind
pinch salt
120 ml (¼ pint or ½ cup) water
120 ml (¼ pint or ½ cup) yogourt
3 egg yolks

Topping:

3 egg whites

3 tablespoons sugar

Blend together the sugar, cornflour, lemon juice and rind, salt, water and yogourt. Cook in a double saucepan until the mixture thickens, stirring all the time. Cool slightly and beat in the egg yolks. Pour into pastry case. Whisk egg whites and sugar to stiff peaks. Pile on top of filling. Bake in a slow oven pre-heated to 165°C (325°F or Gas Mark 3) until the meringue is crisp and golden. (About 15 minutes.)

LIME MERINGUE PIE

6–8 Servings

240 grs (8 oz) short crust pastry (i.e. using half the quantity of recipe (p. 181)
30 grs (1 oz or 3 tablespoons) cornflour
120 grs (4 oz or ½ cup) granulated sugar
water

3 egg yolks
75 ml (2½ oz or 5 tablespoons) strained fresh lime juice
1 dessertspoon grated lime peel
pinch salt
3 stiffly beaten egg whites
60 grs (2 oz or ¼ cup) castor sugar

Line a flan ring with pastry, prick the base finely and bake the pie case 'blind' (p. 185).

Mix cornflour with granulated sugar and dilute with 1 dcl (1 gill or ½ cup) warm water. Lightly beat the yolks and stir into cornflour and sugar mixture. Then, little by little, dilute with 360 ml (12 oz or 1½ cups) boiling water. Blend well, cook over hot water for 5–6 minutes, stirring all the time. Remove from heat, add lime juice, peel and salt. Allow to cool slightly, pour into pastry case. Fold castor sugar a tablespoon at a time into the whites, pile on top of the lime filling, dredge with a little castor sugar and bake in a moderate oven 190°C (375°F or Gas Mark 4) for 10–12 minutes, till the top is set and golden.

FLORIDA LIME PIE

6–8 Servings

1 tablespoon gelatine
4 tablespoons cold water
240 gr (8 oz or 1 cup) sugar
120 ml (¼ pint or ½ cup) lime juice*
grated zest of one lime

⅛ teaspoon salt
4 yolks
4 eggs whites, 1 beaten stiff
one 22 cm (9 inch) pie (tart) shell baked 'blind' (p. 185)

Soak gelatine in cold water while you cook 120 grs (4 oz or ½ cup) sugar, lime juice, grated rind, salt and egg yolks in the top of a double boiler, stirring constantly until the consistency of a custard is reached. Add gelatine to hot custard, stir well. Beat remaining sugar into stiffly beaten egg whites. Fold hot custard carefully into egg whites, stir to cool, pour into baked pie shell and chill before serving.

* Only fresh lime juice should be used.

CRÈME DE MENTHE TART (PIE)

6 Servings

1 tablespoon gelatine
4 tablespoons cold water
4 egg yolks
180 grs (6 oz or ¾ cup) sugar
4–5 tablespoons crème de menthe liqueur

360 ml (12 oz or 1½ cups) double cream
25 cm (10 inch) tart case baked blind (p. 185)
4 tablespoons shredded coconut

Soften gelatine in cold water, then dissolve over simmering water. Beat yolks with sugar until light and fluffy. Blend in gelatine into the yolk and sugar mixture. Add crème de menthe and stir well. Whip the cream until firm, fold into the mixture, put into tart case, sprinkle the top with coconut and chill overnight.

FRENCH CHERRY TART (PIE)

6–8 Servings

tart pastry (pp. 181–3)
½ kg (1 lb or 2½ cups) stoned cherries

120 grs (4 oz or ½ cup) sugar
3 tablespoons redcurrant jelly (p. 214)

Pre-heat oven to 220°C (425°F or Gas Mark 6). Line a tart case with pastry. Put in a layer of cherries, sprinkle with sugar. Finish off with a layer of cherries showing least sign of stoning damage. Bake for 35 minutes. Spoon redcurrant jelly over cherries, put back in the oven for 5 minutes. Remove, allow to cool and serve.

PEAR TART (PIE)

6–8 Servings

puff pastry (pp. 181–2)	1 teaspoon cinnamon
confectioners' custard (p. 187)	1 teaspoon nutmeg
4 pears	1–2 tablespoons butter
4 tablespoons sugar	

Line a tart tin with pastry and put in refrigerator until needed. Have the custard ready and pre-heat oven to 235°C (450°F or Gas Mark 7). Peel pears, cut in half, scoop out core. Mix sugar, cinnamon and nutmeg.

Sprinkle tart case with half the sugar and spice mixture. Put one half pear, core side down, in the middle and arrange the rest around it in a circle. Cover with custard, sprinkle with remaining spiced sugar, dot with small pieces of butter and bake for 15 minutes. Reduce heat to 205°C (400°F or Gas Mark 5), bake for another 12–15 minutes. Cool and serve.

DATE MERINGUE TART (PIE)

6 Servings

tart pastry (pp. 181–3)	60 grs (2 oz or $\frac{2}{3}$ cup) ground almonds
120 grs (4 oz or $\frac{1}{2}$ cup) large stoned dates	120 grs (4 or $\frac{1}{2}$ cup) castor sugar
1 tablespoon brandy	120 grs (4 oz or $\frac{1}{2}$ cup) castor sugar
3 egg whites	

Line a 20 cm (8 inch) tart tin with pastry. Cut each date into four, sprinkle with brandy and leave to macerate for 20 minutes, then drain. Beat the egg whites to a stiff froth and add almonds, sugar and dates. Fill the tart shell with the mixture, bake in a hot oven 235°C (450°F or Gas Mark 7) for 25–30 minutes, sprinkle with castor sugar and serve hot.

ALMOND TARTLETS

6 Servings

sugar pastry (p. 181)
180 grs (6 oz or 1½ cups) toasted slivered almonds
240 grs (8 oz or 1 cup) sugar

¼ litre (½pint or 1 cup) double cream
1 tablespoon Grand Marnier or other liqueur

Line small round or oval shaped (barquette) tartlet tins with pastry. Pre-heat oven to 205° C (400°F or Gas Mark 5). Combine almonds, sugar, cream and Grand Marnier and spoon the mixture into tartlets. Bake for 12–15 minutes and serve warm.

STRAWBERRY BARQUETTES

Barquettes, as the name implies, are boat-shaped little tartlets, so popular in France as a dessert. They are particularly good heaped with wild strawberries.

Using oval shaped tartlet tins, proceed exactly as described in recipe for cherry barquettes substituting strawberries, wild if possible, for cherries.

CHERRY BARQUETTES

Tart Pastry (pp. 181–3)
butter

½ kg (1 lb) stoned cherries
melted redcurrant jelly (p. 214)

Make the tart pastry of your choice and let it rest. Butter tartlet tins.

Pre-heat oven to 205°C (400°F or Gas Mark 5).

Roll and cut the pastry and line the barquette tins. Prick the pastry with a fork.

Bake 10 minutes. Remove from oven and cool. Remove the tarts from the tins. Fill with cherries and cover with a teaspoon of redcurrant jelly which should be cool and semi-liquid.

Fritters

RUSSIAN WHITE ACACIA FRITTERS

White acacia blossoms
pancake batter (p. 185)

fat or oil for deep frying
castor sugar

Rinse acacia blossoms (these must be of the white variety, as yellow ones are poisonous), dip in batter, holding by the stem, drop into boiling fat, allow to fry for a few seconds, drain on absorbent kitchen paper, sprinkle with castor sugar and serve.

ELDER BLOSSOM FRITTERS

As above.

SOUFFLÉ FRITTERS

½ litre (1 pint or 2 cups) water
6 tablespoons butter
½ teaspoon salt
1½ teaspoons sugar
375 grs (12 oz or 3 cups) sifted flour

6 eggs
1 tablespoon rum or brandy
oil or fat for deep frying
icing sugar
Apricot sauce (p. 193)

Put water, butter, salt and sugar into a saucepan and bring to a boil. Remove from heat, mix in flour, put the saucepan back on the fire, and stir with a wooden spoon until paste comes away from the sides of the saucepan. Remove from heat. One by one, add the eggs, stirring vigorously. The paste should be very smooth. Flavour with rum, brandy or other liqueur to taste. Take up spoonfuls the size of a walnut and drop them one at a time into hot, deep fat. (Slip paste from the spoon with the blade of a knife dipped in hot water.) When fritters double their size and have a fine light golden colour, remove, and drain on a cloth. Sprinkle with icing sugar. Serve Apricot Sauce separately.

SOMERSET APPLE FRITTERS

6–8 Servings

6 large ripe eating apples
juice of 1–2 lemons
1 cup flour
1 teaspoon salt
2 tablespoons sugar
2 tablespoons milk

2 raw yolks
2 tablespoons melted butter
2 egg whites
oil or other fat for deep frying
icing sugar

Wash and core the apples, slice into rings and put them in the lemon juice. Sift flour, salt and sugar together into a bowl. Add milk, egg yolks and melted butter. Beat until smooth. Whip egg whites to stiff peaks and fold into the batter. Dip each apple ring into the batter and deep fry in hot oil until golden brown. (For all deep frying and dumpling making, we find a chip basket very useful.) Drain, sprinkle with icing sugar.

CANARY ISLAND APPLE FRITTERS

6 Servings

6 tablespoons sugar
6 tablespoons water
6 apples 750 grs (1½ lb)
375 grs (12 oz) sifted flour
⅛ teaspoon salt

3 tablespoons brandy
2 stiffly beaten whites of egg
oil for frying
1 tablespoon icing sugar

Prepare the syrup using 6 tablespoons sugar and equal amount of water. Peel and grate the apples. Mix flour with the syrup, add seasoning, brandy, apple and whites of egg. Mix well and, taking a spoonful at a time, fry in oil. Drain, sprinkle with icing sugar and serve.

BALEARIC BANANAS

6 Servings

4 tablespoons flour
60 ml (2 oz or ¼ cup) water
small pinch of salt
120 ml (4 oz or ½ cup) red wine

4 tablespoons olive oil
6 bananas
castor sugar

Mix a smooth batter of flour with water, salt and red wine (the red wine gives an interesting 'different' colour to the sweet), making sure that there are no lumps. Heat olive oil in a frying-pan. While the oil is being heated, slice the bananas into the batter. Taking a tablespoon of batter with 4 or 5 slices of banana in each, drop them into the oil. Fry until golden (be very careful not to burn them), then turn and fry the other side. Squeeze each fritter lightly between two forks to drain them of surplus oil. Serve with a sprinkling of castor sugar.

POTATO BUÑUELOS

6 Servings

6 large cooked potatoes	2 tablespoons butter
½ teaspoon salt	2 beaten eggs
¼ teaspoon pepper	oil for frying

Mash the potatoes, season and mix with butter and eggs. With a teaspoon, drop a small quantity of the mixture into hot oil, deep fry, drain and serve with sugar or a dessert sauce (pp. 193–5).

BUÑUELOS IN SYRUP

Prepare potato buñuelos (see above), fry and drain. Make a light syrup (p. 217), immerse the buñuelos in it and serve.

APRICOT OR PLUM FRITTERS STUFFED WITH ALMONDS

150 grs (5 oz or 1¼ cups) flour	120 grs (4 oz or ½ cup) castor
1 raw yolk	sugar
¼ teaspoon salt	blanched almonds
120 ml (4 oz or ½ cup) beer	fat for deep frying
1 teaspoon brandy	vanilla sugar
1 kg (2 lb) apricots (or plums)	

Make a light batter using flour, yolk, salt, beer and brandy. Stir until smooth and allow to stand for 2–3 hours.

Wash and dry apricots but do not cut. Heat the castor sugar in a pan with a tablespoon water. As soon as sugar dissolves into syrup, put in apricots, simmer gently for 7–8 minutes and remove from heat. Drain apricots and leave to cool. Taking care not to break them, extract stones, fill each apricot with as many almonds as it will take comfortably.

Put fat to heat. Dip each apricot in batter, deep fry until golden brown and drain on absorbent paper. Sprinkle with vanilla sugar and serve hot.

To have vanilla sugar always on hand, keep 1–2 vanilla beans in a 500 grs (1 lb) jar of sugar. Top up as you take out vanilla flavoured sugar and make sure the jar has a well-fitting lid.

BEOLAS

These are traditional Tunisian Passover fritters for which matzo meal is used instead of flour. They make an interesting dessert, reminiscent of baba, impregnated with jasmine or orange blossom-flavoured syrup or honey. They are very easy to make and the preparation takes surprisingly little time.

120 grs (4 oz or ½ cup) sugar
120 ml (4 oz or ½ cup) water
1 teaspoon grated lemon rind
3 eggs
2 tablespoons fine matzo meal

2 tablespoons ground almonds
oil for deep frying
few drops jasmine essence or
   orange blossom water

Heat sugar and water to dissolve, add lemon rind and boil for 4–5 minutes. Strain.

Beat eggs, add matzo meal and almonds and mix well. Heat oil, drop mixture in spoonfuls, fry until lightly browned on all sides. Drain on absorbent kitchen paper, put in a glass dish.

Add jasmine essence or orange blossom water to syrup, pour over fritters, cool, chill and serve.

RICE FRITTERS

Using cooled dessert rice (p. 66), make sweet fritters by dropping a tablespoon of the rice mixture into hot oil and deep frying until golden on both sides. Drain well. Sprinkle with sugar and serve.

Variations:
1. Add ground almonds to rice, cook as described and serve with sprinkling of sugar and cinnamon.
2. Mix rice with grated raw apple and serve sprinkled with brown sugar.
3. Mix rice with equal amount of cottage cheese, fry and coat with shredded coconut.

COPRA SAMOSAS (COCONUT SAMOSAS)

In India these samosas are served as sweetmeats. One of the favourite fillings is freshly made mint chutney (p. 215).

6 Servings
dough for samosas (see p. 186)
syrup for jalebis (see p. 199)
480 grs (1 lb or 6 cups) shredded
   coconut
6 crushed cardamom seeds
90 grs (3 oz or 1 cup) ground
   almonds

60 grs (2 oz or 6 tablespoons)
   raisins
120 grs (4 oz or ½ cup) sugar
a few tablespoons milk
ghee (p. 221) or oil for deep
   frying
slivered pistachio nuts

Prepare the dough as described. Make the syrup and keep warm in a pan of hot water.

Combine coconut, cardamom, almonds, raisins and sugar. Mix well, bind with a little milk.

Roll out the dough very thin and cut into $5\frac{3}{4}$–$7\frac{1}{2}$ cm ($2\frac{1}{2}$–3 inches) squares, put a generous teaspoon of the stuffing in each square, leaving the edges clear. Brush the edges with a little milk or water, fold corner to corner to make a triangle, and press well to seal the edges.

Heat fat and deep fry a few samosas at a time until golden brown on both sides. Drain, dip each samosa in syrup, decorate with a sprinkling of pistachio slivers and arrange on a dish.

Dessert Dumplings

MIRKA'S FRUIT DUMPLINGS

Two Czech students, Mirka and Jiri, came to stay with me one summer and made my mouth water with the descriptions of Mirka's mother's fruit dumplings. Mirka thought she could remember how they were made, so the three of us started up a conveyor belt in the kitchen. Jiri, hulled and washed strawberries. Mirka made the dough and I put water on and put yoghourt through the blender to substitute for sour cream. The results were a nasty, pasty, soggy mess, which we ate miserably reassuring each other that 'they weren't all that bad – really...' Mirka wrote to her mother about our failure and a letter came back by return post with the explanation: we had left out the potatoes. We started up our conveyor belt again that evening and the dumplings were delicious. We ate fruit dumplings for a week after that and only stopped because the sun suddenly came out and Mirka and I could hardly get into our bathing costumes. Now, whenever Mirka writes from Prague, she often encloses one of her mother's recipes. I owe all my Czech recipes to her. (T.L.)

6–8 Servings

2 large cold boiled potatoes
120 grs (4 oz or 1 cup) flour
pinch salt
1 egg

8 tablespoons milk
fruit: whole plums or strawberries
castor sugar
sour cream

Rub potatoes through a sieve and mix with flour and salt. Make a well in the middle and add egg and milk. Work into a stiff dough. Roll out fairly thinly on to a floured board and cut into 7½ cm (3 inch) squares. Place fruit in middle of each square and roll into a ball. Cook for 5–8 minutes in slightly salted boiling water. Serve sprinkled with castor sugar and eat with sour cream.

CZECH RASPBERRY YEAST DUMPLINGS

6–8 Servings

10 grs (⅓ oz or ¾ cake) baker's
yeast
sugar
2½ dcl (½ pint or 1 cup) milk
240 grs (8 oz or 2¼ cups) sifted
flour

¼ kg (½ lb) fine semolina
1 egg
½ teaspoon salt
½ kg (1 lb) raspberries
cottage cheese

Mix the yeast with 4 tablespoons sugar and 2–3 tablespoons warm milk, and leave to rise. Add to the flour. Mix in semolina, the rest of the warmed milk, egg and salt. Beat energetically, then leave in a warm place (airing cupboard is great) for an hour.

On a floured board, roll dough into a long sausage and cut off small pieces, enough to wrap nicely around 4 raspberries. When all the dumplings are ready, put a big saucepan of water on to boil. The time this takes allows the dumplings to settle. Throw them into the boiling water and cook for 8–10 minutes, turning over once. Remove from water, drain and prick with a fork to allow steam to escape. Serve sprinkled with sugar and crumbled cottage cheese.

This recipe is equally successful with apricots or plums.

VARENIKI

This type of dumpling is an Ukrainian speciality. Also popular throughout Russia and in Israel.

6–8 Servings

noodle paste (p. 185)
½ kg (1 lb or 2 cups) cream cheese
2 eggs
1–2 tablespoons sugar

½ teaspoon salt
½ litre (1 pint or 2 cups) sour
cream
pinch cinnamon

Prepare noodle paste as descibed.

Combine cream cheese, eggs, sugar, salt, 4 tablespoons sour cream and cinnamon and mix well.

Roll out dough, cut into small squares. Fill each square with a spoonful of cream cheese, fold into triangles and seal up the edges then bring corners together and pinch, (or cut dough with a round pastry cutter into small circles, fill with cheese, fold and shape into semicircles).

Drop a few at a time into boiling salted water, allowing boiling to be re-established before adding any more. Boil for 10 minutes or until the vareniki rise to the surface.

Remove with a perforated spoon and serve piping hot with sour cream and sugar. Vareniki can also be served with melted butter.

VARENIKI WITH CHERRIES

6–8 Servings

1 kg (2 lb) cherries
180 grs (6 oz or ¾ cup) sugar

Egg noodle paste (p. 185)
sour cream

Stone the cherries, preserving all the juice, add sugar and leave for 3–4 hours. Crush five or six cherry stones into fine powder, add to the cherries, cover with 2 dcl (½ pint or 1 cup) water, bring to the boil, simmer for 1 or 2 minutes and strain, keeping all the juice. Roll out the dough as described and fill each little circle with two or three cherries. Cook, remove with a perforated spoon, put in a heated serving dish and keep warm.

Boil down the strained juice left over from the cherries and allow to cool. Serve this syrupy sauce and sour cream with the vareniki.

VARENIKI WITH PRUNES

6–8 Servings

600 grs (1¼ lb or 3 cups) prunes
60 grs (2 oz or 4 tablespoons)
  sugar

egg noodle paste (p. 185)
castor sugar

Boil the prunes in a little water, rub through a sieve, add sugar, simmer together to thicken the mixture and allow to cool. Roll out the paste, fill with prune purée and cook as described. Sprinkle with castor sugar and serve with sour cream.

Pancakes, Crêpes

PANNEQUETS A L'IMPÉRATRICE

6–8 Servings

250 grs (8 oz or 2 cups) sifted flour
8 egg yolks
½ litre (1 pint or 2 cups) milk
120 ml (4 oz or ½ cup) cream
4 tablespoons sugar
pinch salt
120 grs (4 oz or ½ cup) softened butter
½ teaspoon vanilla extract
8 stiffly beaten egg whites
6–8 tablespoons whipped cream
dessert rice (p. 66)
Maraschino
pears in syrup (p. 56)

Put the flour in a bowl, add yolks one by one, dilute with milk, adding a little at a time. Add cream, sugar, salt and softened butter. Blend in vanilla. Allow to stand for 3 hours. Just before frying the pannequets, fold in egg whites.

Butter the griddle or frying pan and fry very thin pancakes, taking care to spread the batter in the pan evenly. Turn, and when done, keep the pancakes piled on top of each other until all are ready.

Separate the pancakes.

Spread with dessert rice, mixed while hot with whipped cream flavoured with Maraschino. Top with diced pears cooked in syrup and sprinkled with Maraschino. Fold the pannequets over, arrange on a round dish in a circle, overlapping them slightly. Sprinkle with fine granulated sugar and put under the grill (broiler) for one minute to glaze the surface. Fill the middle of the dish with halved pears poached in Maraschino-flavoured syrup and well-drained.

If desired, cover the pears with a few tablespoons of chocolate sauce (p. 194) added to the syrup in which the pears were poached.

JAM PANNEQUETS

Make pannequets as described. Spread them with a layer of jam and fold over. Arrange in a circle on a dish, sprinkle with fine sugar, put under the grill for one minute to glaze. The centre of the dish may be filled with fruit poached in syrup and drained. Flavour the sauce with Kirsch or other liqueur and serve separately.

PANNEQUETS WITH FRANGIPANE CREAM

Spread each pannequet with one tablespoon Frangipane Cream (p. 188). Fold, sprinkle with sugar, and glaze for one minute under the grill.

CRÊPES SUZETTE

10 Servings
batter for crêpes (p. 185)   orange butter (p. 189)
brandy

Make the crêpe batter and add 2 tablespoons brandy. Cook 20 paper thin pancakes.

Butter a metal serving dish and heat it slightly. Spread the crêpes with the orange butter, fold in quarters and arrange on the heated platter.

Heat 5 tablespoons of brandy in a small pan and pour it over the crêpes. Ignite and serve at once.

CRÊPES WITH CHESTNUT PURÉE

4–6 Servings
batter for crêpes (p. 185)   apricot jam (p. 213)
chestnut purée (p. 24)   90 grs (3 oz) slivered almonds

Fry 12 crêpes, spread each one with the chestnut purée and roll up. Melt the jam and spoon it over the rolled crêpes. Brown the slivered almonds lightly in a dry frying pan, sprinkle over crêpes and serve.

CRÊPES WITH COINTREAU FLAMBÉES

4–6 Servings
batter for crêpes (p. 185)
360 ml (¾ pint or 1½ cup)
confectioners' custard (p. 187)

120 ml (¼ pint or ½ cup) Cointreau
4 tablespoons sugar

Cook twelve crêpes, i.e. very thin pancakes, keep them hot in a dish over hot water.

Add 4 tablespoons Cointreau to custard.

Spread the custard on the crêpes and roll them up. Place on a heated serving dish. Sprinkle with sugar. Just before serving heat the remaining Cointreau, pour over crêpes, ignite and serve at once.

Waffles

GAUFRES / FRENCH WAFFLES

6 Servings

15 grs ($\frac{1}{2}$ oz or 1 cake) fresh yeast
or 2$\frac{1}{2}$ teaspoons dry yeast
120 ml (4 oz or $\frac{1}{2}$ cup) warm
water
240 grs (8 oz or 2 cups) sifted
flour

$\frac{1}{2}$ teaspoon salt
60 grs (2 oz or $\frac{1}{4}$ cup) sugar
240 ml ($\frac{1}{2}$ pint or 1 cup) cream
2 tablespoons butter
chantilly – whipped cream
(p. 189)

Dilute yeast in water, stir in 6 tablespoons flour and leave to rise and double in volume. Add remaining flour, salt and sugar. Heat cream, dilute butter in it and blend the mixture into flour. Work the batter for 7–8 minutes, leave in a warm place for 2–2$\frac{1}{2}$ hours.

Spread some mixture in hot waffle iron, close and cook. Continue until all batter is used up. Serve with crème chantilly.

CANADIAN WAFFLES

6 Servings

240 grs (8 oz or 2 cups) sifted
flour
$\frac{1}{2}$ teaspoon salt
1 level tablespoon baking powder

2 eggs
$\frac{1}{2}$ litre (1 pint or 2 cups) milk
butter
hot maple syrup

Mix flour with salt and baking powder. Separate eggs, beat yolks, dilute with milk and blend into flour. Add 75 grs (2$\frac{1}{2}$ oz or 5 tablespoons) melted butter and stir well.

Beat egg whites into stiff foam, fold into batter. Cook in waffle irons and serve with butter and hot maple syrup.

RUSSIAN CHOCOLATE WAFFLES

4–6 Servings

4 eggs	120 grs (4 oz or 1 cup) flour
2 tablespoons sugar	180 ml (6 oz or ¾ cup) milk
3 tablespoons melted butter	oil or butter for greasing irons
¼ teaspoon salt	whipped cream (p. 189)
60 grs (2 oz or ½ cup) grated chocolate	

Separate the yolks from the whites, blend the yolks with sugar, melted butter, salt, chocolate and flour. Slowly add the milk and mix thoroughly. Just before frying, add stiffly beaten whites. Cook (p. 125) and serve with whipped cream.

Petits Fours, Biscuits

SPONGE FINGERS

To make 2 dozen

3 eggs	30 grs (1 oz or 2 tablespoons) butter
90 grs (3 oz or 6 tablespoons) sugar	
90 grs (3 oz or ¾ cup) plain flour	30 grs (1 oz or 2 tablespoons) castor sugar

Separate eggs and beat yolks with the sugar. Beat egg whites until stiff and fold into yolk and sugar mixture. Fold in flour. Fill a piping bag with this mixture and pipe 'fingers' on to a buttered floured baking tray. Leave for a few minutes, then sprinkle with castor sugar. Let sugar soak in for a few minutes then bake in a moderate oven pre-heated to 190°C (375°F or Gas Mark 4) for 15 minutes.

LANGUES DE CHAT (CAT'S TONGUES)

120 grs (4 oz or ½ cup) butter	3 eggs separated
4 tablespoons sugar	120 grs (4 oz or ½ cup) sifted cake flour
1 tablespoon vanilla sugar (p. 113) or ½ teaspoon vanilla extract	

Beat the butter in a warm bowl, add sugar and vanilla flavoured sugar. Work the mixture until it becomes creamy, then mix in egg yolks, one by one. Carefully add flour and fold in stiffly beaten whites of egg. Line a baking sheet with heavy waxed paper and, using a forcing bag with a round nozzle, pipe the mixture to make little strips about 2½ cm (1 inch) apart. Bake in the oven pre-heated to 205°C (400°F or Gas Mark 5) for 7–8 minutes, or until biscuits are pale golden with slightly darker edges. Remove from baking tin before they are completely cold. Keep in an air-tight tin.

127

TUILES WITH ALMONDS

45 grs (1½ oz or ½ cup) blanched,
  pounded almonds
½ teaspoon potato flour
180 grs (6 oz or ¾ cup) sugar
2 egg whites

1 teaspoon vanilla flavoured sugar
  (p. 113) or ½ teaspoon vanilla
  extract
1 egg yolk
shredded almonds

Blend pounded almonds with potato flour, sugar and one egg white. When the mixture is smooth and creamy, add vanilla and the egg yolk. Mix and add the second egg white. The mixture should be soft and easy to spread. If it appears to be a little too firm, add a little more egg white.

Using a forcing bag with a plain nozzle, pipe the mixture on to a buttered baking sheet in little balls the size of a walnut, leaving a space of about 5 cm (2½ inch) between them. Pre-heat oven to 135°C (275°F or Gas Mark 1). Sprinkle each with a small pinch of shredded almond and bake until golden. While still warm, bend each one over a rolling pin, giving it a slightly curved shape.

BRANDY SNAPS

Makes 2–3 dozen

120 grs (4 oz or ½ cup) sugar
120 grs (4 oz or ½ cup) butter
120 grs (4 oz or ⅓ cup) golden
  syrup

120 grs (4 oz or 1 cup) plain flour
1 teaspoon powdered ginger

In a heavy based pan, heat the sugar, butter and golden syrup until it barely comes to the boil. Remove from heat. Stir in the flour and ginger. Mix well. Pre-heat oven to 190°C (375°F or Gas Mark 4).

Drop the mixture on to buttered baking trays, easing the drops into neat round. Leave plenty of space – about 5–6 cm (2½ inch) round each drop to allow for spreading. Bake for 6–8 minutes until they are flat and brown and bubbly. Allow to cool for a minute then lift each brandy snap with a spatula and wrap round the thick handle of a wooden spoon into a roll. Leave for a few minutes, then ease off and leave on a wire rack to cool.
Store in an airtight tin.

Before serving, fill with brandy flavoured whipped cream (p. 189).

COCONUT KISSES

Makes 3 dozen

4 egg whites
300 grs (10 oz or 1¼ cups) castor
  sugar

240 grs (8 oz or 3 cups)
  desiccated coconut

Beat egg whites until they form stiff peaks. Fold in sugar and the coconut. Drop mixture on to greaseproof paper on a baking sheet, leaving plenty of room for kisses to expand. Pre-heat oven to 150°C (300°F or Gas Mark 2). Bake for 40 minutes or until they are pale golden. Cool on a wire rack, then remove from paper. Serve with ices.

BARBADOS COOKIES

(To eat with ices)

Makes 5–6 dozen

½ kg (1 lb or 2 cups) butter
½ kg (1 lb or 2 cups) soft brown sugar

250 grs (8 oz or 2 cups) flour
2 eggs

Cream the butter and sugar together, mix in the flour and add the eggs one at a time, beating after each one. Chill in the refrigerator until the mixture can be cut cleanly with a knife. Using two teaspoons, drop little lumps of this paste onto buttered greaseproof paper on a baking sheet, leaving space between each drop to allow for spreading. Bake for 15 minutes in the oven pre-heated to 175°C (350°F or Gas Mark 3). Cool on a wire rack before removing from paper. Store in an airtight tin somewhere out of reach preferably high up, so if you can't resist these biscuits, at least you get some exercise as you nibble.

Variations:
Before baking, press a half walnut or an almond into each cookie.
Or:
When cool, dip cookies quickly into melted chocolate, so they emerge as half moons – half in night, half in day.

OPORTO WALNUT DROPS

To make 2 dozen

180 grs (6 oz or ¾ cup) butter
180 grs (6 oz or ¾ cup) sugar
⅛ teaspoon salt
180 grs (6 oz or 1½ cups) flour

60 grs (2 oz or ¼ cup) port
90 grs (3 oz or ¾ cup) finely chopped walnuts

Pre-heat oven to 175°C (350°F or Gas Mark 3). Cream butter with sugar, add salt and incorporate flour, moistening it with port as you mix. Add walnuts, stir well. Drop small teaspoons of mixture on greased baking sheet and bake for 20–25 minutes.

HAZELNUT FINGERS

360 grs (12 oz or 1½ cups) sugar
90 grs (3 oz or 1 cup) ground hazelnuts
2 eggs
1½ tablespoons sherry

180 grs (6 oz or 1¾ cups) pastry flour
60 grs (2 oz or 4 tablespoons) melted butter
90 grs (3 oz or ½ cup) semi-sweet chocolate

Put sugar and hazelnuts into a bowl, add eggs and sherry and mix well. Add flour, then stir in butter, which should be melted but not hot.

Tear off small pieces of pastry, roll into little fingers. Pre-heat oven to 175°C (350°F or Gas Mark 3).

Lightly grease a baking sheet, put hazelnut fingers on it and bake for about 15 minutes. Remove and leave on a rack to cool. Melt chocolate in a bowl over hot water. Dip one end of each finger in it and stand upside down to dry.

WALNUT MACAROONS

This recipe originates in Ukraine. Unlike other macaroons the mixture for these is first cooked in a double saucepan, then baked.

2 eggs whites
180 grs (6 oz or ¾ cup) sugar
½ tablespoon lemon juice

240 grs (8 oz or 2 cups) chopped walnuts
3 tablespoons shelled pine kernels

Put egg whites with sugar and lemon juice in the top of a double saucepan and start cooking over simmering water, whisking all the time. Cook in this manner for 10 minutes. Add walnuts, stir well, cook for 5 minutes and remove. Pre-heat oven to 175°C (350°F or Gas Mark 3).

Lightly grease a baking sheet. Take a spoonful of the walnut mixture at a time and drop on to baking sheet without allowing the macaroons to touch.

Stud each with a few pine kernels and bake until the macaroons set and turn pale golden.

To make almond macaroons, substitute almonds for walnuts.

IRAQI PEPPERY MACAROONS

240 grs (8 oz or 2 cups) plain
   flour
1 teaspoon baking powder
240 grs (8 oz or 1 cup) sugar
pinch freshly grated black pepper
1 teaspoon ground cinnamon
½ teaspoon ground cloves

½ teaspoon ground nutmeg
4 tablespoons candied peel
   (p. 205)
1 teaspoon grated lemon rind
3 eggs
1–2 tablespoons butter
icing sugar

Combine flour, baking powder, sugar, pepper, cinnamon, cloves and nutmeg in a mixing bowl.

Chop candied peel and add to dry ingredients together with lemon rind. Beat eggs, put in mixing bowl and mix well. Grease a baking sheet with butter and rub some in the palms of your hands Pinch off pieces of dough, roll into balls the size of a walnut, place on baking sheet and leave to dry overnight.

Pre-heat over to 150°C (300°F or Gas Mark 2). Bake the macaroons for 25–30 minutes, until they brown. Sprinkle with icing sugar, cool and store in an air-tight tin for 10–15 days for the macaroons to mellow.

ORIENTAL SESAME BISCUITS

240 grs (8 oz or 2¼ cups) flour
1 teaspoon salt
90 grs (3 oz or 9 tablespoons)
   toasted sesame seeds

180 grs (6 oz or ¾ cup)
   shortening
60 ml (2 oz or 4 tablespoons)
   strained orange juice

Combine flour, salt and sesame seeds in a mixing bowl. Add shortening. First cut it into the flour, then rub lightly with finger tips until the mixture begins to look like fine breadcrumbs. Little by little mix in orange juice and knead lightly. Roll out pastry to a thickness of ¾ cm (¼ inch). Cut into oblongs 5 cm (2½ inch) long and 2½ cm (1 inch) wide. Put the cut biscuits on ungreased baking sheet. Bake in a moderately hot oven, pre-heated to 250°C (400°F or Gas Mark 5) for about 15 minutes, until the biscuits are golden brown. Take off baking sheet, and leave on a wire rack to cool.

Dessert Omelettes

RUM OMELETTE

4 Servings

5 eggs	1 tablespoon butter
2 teaspoons sugar	castor sugar
3 tablespoons rum	1 tablespoon warm rum

Beat eggs with sugar, add rum gradually, and beat into a froth. Heat butter in pan, add beaten eggs, cook omelette in the usual manner, transfer to a heated serving dish and sprinkle with sugar. Warm rum, pour over omelette, ignite and serve at once.

OMELETTE NORMANDE

2 Generous servings

2 medium-sized, peeled, cored chopped apples	3 tablespoons Calvados
1½ tablespoons vanilla-flavoured sugar (p. 113)	4 eggs
3 tablespoons butter	3 tablespoons castor sugar
	pinch salt

Cook the apples with vanilla sugar in 2 tablespoons butter until they are very soft. Add 1 tablespoon Calvados. Beat eggs with 1½ tablespoons castor sugar, 2 tablespoons water and a pinch of salt. Heat remaining butter in an omelette pan and pour in the eggs. Stir once or twice with the flat of a wooden fork, lift the edges to let the liquid part run under and shake the pan to keep the omelette free. When it is set but still creamy, spread the apple mixture in the centre, fold over, turn the omelette out on to a flameproof dish, sprinkle with sugar and glaze the surface under a hot grill. Take to the table at once, pour over the omelette 2 tablespoons warm Calvados and ignite it.

SOUFFLÉ OMELETTE

4–6 Servings
  240 grs (8 oz or 1 cup) castor
    sugar
  6 egg yolks
  flavouring (vanilla, coffee, choco-
    late, grated lemon or orange
    rind, various liqueurs)

8 stiffly beaten egg whites
1 tablespoon butter
icing sugar

Blend sugar and yolks with chosen flavouring in a bowl, until the mixture turns white and begins to form a ribbon. Carefully fold in the whites. Pour the omelette mixture into a long oven-proof dish, buttered and sprinkled with fine sugar. Pile it into a dome, smooth the surface with a knife, decorate by piping some of the mixture through a forcing bag, sprinkle with icing sugar and bake in a hot oven 233°C (450°F or Gas Mark 7) for 16–18 minutes.

OMELETTE WITH SUGAR

Beat the eggs together with sugar and a very small pinch of salt, and cook as an ordinary omelette. Sprinkle it with fine sugar and either make a criss-cross pattern with a special glazing iron or glaze under a grill. Flavour as desired, with grated orange, lemon or tangerine rind.

STRAWBERRY OMELETTE

Make an omelette, beating the eggs with sugar to taste, a small pinch of salt and 2–3 tablespoons cream. Fold in the strawberries, previously steeped in rum or kirsch and sugar. Sprinkle the omelette with fine sugar and glaze under the grill. Surround with crushed strawberries, sprinkled with sugar and flavoured with liqueur.

JAM AND FRUIT OMELETTE

Beat the eggs with castor sugar to taste and a small pinch of salt. Fry the omelette in butter in the usual manner. Fill with the fruit indicated in individual recipes, making sure in the case of cooked fruit that it is well drained. Add a spoonful of appropriate jam if the fruit needs binding. Fold as described, arrange the omelette on a dish sprinkle with castor sugar, and make a criss-cross pattern with a glazing iron or glaze quickly under the grill.

OMELETTE CÉLESTINE

This is a combination of three small omelettes, filled with apricot jam, arranged in a row on a long dish sprinkled with castor sugar and glazed in a hot oven.

OMELETTE REINE PEDAUQUE

Beat the eggs with powdered sugar, fresh cream and some ground almonds, and make two flat omelettes. Put one of these in an oven-proof dish, spread it with a thick layer of apple purée mixed with fresh cream and kirsch, cover with the second omelette and then coat the whole with a layer of meringue (p. 95). Sprinkle with icing sugar and put in a very hot oven until the meringue sets and is golden.

LIQUEUR OMELETTE FLAMBÉE

Rum omelette is the prototype of these omelettes (p. 132). Beat the eggs with sugar to taste and a small pinch of salt, and cook the omelette in butter, keeping it very creamy. Sprinkle with castor sugar, pour over some warmed rum and ignite it at the moment of serving.

Note : In the same way omelettes can be made with Armagnac, Calvados, brandy, whisky, Kirsch and other spirits.

NORWEGIAN OMELETTE
(or BAKED ALASKA, or SURPRISE OMELETTE)

This is a most rewarding dessert to make, it can be prepared in the morning and safely left in the freezer until the evening. A 10 egg-white Norwegian Omelette will only need five minutes' cooking.

The invention of this omelette is attributed to Count Benjamin Thomas Rumford and to Jean Giroix, who was in charge of the Hôtel de Paris kitchens in Monte Carlo in 1895.

The culinary column of *Liberté* printed a piece by Baron Brissé on 6th June 1866, in which he credited the chef of the Chinese

Mission with the authorship of the surprise omelette.

The column says:

'The chefs of the Celestial Empire have exchanged civilities and information with the chefs of the Grand-Hôtel.' The Grand-Hôtel was opened in 1862 and its first chef's name was Balzac.

The report goes on to describe how delighted the French chef in charge of sweet courses was to have learnt from his Chinese colleague 'the method of baking vanilla and ginger ices in the oven', and gives the following instructions:

'Chill the ice until hard, wrap each in a very light pastry crust and put in the oven.

The pastry is baked before the ice, protected by the pastry shell, can melt.

The gourmets can thus give themselves the double pleasure of biting through hot crust and cooling the palate with the fragrant ices.'

oval-shaped sponge cake (p. 79)
1 tablespoon liqueur (Kirsch, Maraschino, etc.)
¾ litre (1½ pints or 3 cups) ice cream (pp. 163–8)
180 grs (6 oz or 1 cup) soft fruit (strawberries, raspberries, etc.)

ordinary meringue (p. 95) using
  10 egg whites and 180 grs
  (6 oz or ¾ cup) sugar
½ teaspoon cream of tartar
1½ tablespoons chopped almonds
icing sugar

Put the cake on a board covered with foil, scoop out the centre,* leaving a shell 2½ cm (1 inch) thick, and sprinkle with liqueur. Pack the ice cream and fruit in the centre, freeze until very firm. Cover completely with meringue, to which cream of tartar has been added during beating, smooth over the surface to a thickness of 1½ cm (⅔ inch) decorate the omelette by piping some of the meringue mixture through a forcing bag, sprinkle with almonds and leave in the freezer until required.

When you are ready for it, pre-heat the oven to 246°C (470°F or Gas Mark 8), dust the omelette with icing sugar, bake for 5 minutes, which is enough to cook and colour the meringue without melting the ice cream and serve. Alternately, instead of using a foil-covered board, you can put the piece of cake on a long dish, place the ice cream and fruit on top, then cover with meringue and continue as described, but hollowing out the cake into a shell helps the omelette to keep its shape for several hours.

* The scooped out cake crumbs can be used for other desserts. See pp. 22 and 62.

This omelette offers endless possibilities for variation. Here are some classic examples:

NORWEGIAN OMELETTE WITH CHERRIES

Fill the cake shell with a mixture of red currant and raspberry ice cream, garnish with stoned cherries steeped in Kirsch. Cover with meringue, bake as described, surround with well-drained brandied cherries, pour some heated Kirsch over the omelette, ignite it at the table and serve at once while the flames are still playing.

NORWEGIAN OMELETTE WITH PEACHES

As above, using raspberry ice cream and peaches poached in vanilla-flavoured syrup. Cover with Maraschino-flavoured Italian meringue (p. 96), sprinkle with icing sugar and bake as described.

NORWEGIAN OMELETTE WITH PEARS

Proceed as above, adding a layer of pears cooked in syrup to vanilla-flavoured ice cream, before covering it with meringue.

NORWEGIAN OMELETTE WITH PINEAPPLE

Proceed as described, using pineapple ice cream and pineapple cooked in syrup, diced and sprinkled with Kirsch.

NORWEGIAN OMELETTE WITH TANGERINES

Use tangerine-flavoured ice cream and, after baking the omelette, decorate with glazed tangerines.

SURPRISE OMELETTE NEAPOLITAN STYLE

Fill the cake shell with strawberry ice cream and pieces of marrons glacés, cover with Kirsch-flavoured Italian meringue (p. 96), serve with cherries (see recipe for Norwegian Omelette with Cherries Flambée), ignite at table.

SURPRISE OMELETTE WITH VIOLETS

Fill the cake shell with vanilla ice cream studded with crystallised violets, cover with ordinary meringue, decorate with crystallised violets, and bake in the usual way.

Soufflés

KIRSCH SOUFFLÉ

4–5 Servings

Packet of sponge fingers (p. 127)
5 tablespoons Kirsch
75 grs (2½ oz or 7 tablespoons) mixed chopped glacé fruits
60 grs (2 oz or 4 tablespoons) butter

30 grs (1 oz or 4 tablespoons) flour
1 dcl (1 gill or ½ cup) milk
60 grs (2 oz or 4 tablespoons) sugar
3 raw egg yolks
3 stiffly beaten egg whites

Sprinkle sponge fingers with 1 tablespoon Kirsch. Do the same with glacé fruits on a separate plate. Butter a soufflé dish and heat oven to 233°C (450°F or Gas Mark 7). Melt butter, add flour and blend well. Remove from heat, gradually stir in milk, return to heat and cook for 5 minutes. Cool slightly, beat in sugar, egg yolks and remaining Kirsch, then fold in egg whites. Pour half the mixture into the dish, cover lightly with a layer of sponge fingers and fruit, pour on the rest of the souffle mixture, Bake first in a hot oven 233°C (450°F or Gas Mark 7) for 15 minutes, then lower to 190°C (375°F or Gas Mark 4) and bake for 30 minutes. Serve at once.

GRAND MARNIER SOUFFLÉ

4–5 Servings

120 grs (4 oz or ½ cup) sugar
½ litre (1 pint or 2 cups) milk
60 grs (2 oz or 4 tablespoons) butter
45 grs (1½ oz or 6 tablespoons) flour

5 fresh egg yolks
8 whites of egg
1 large liqueur glass of Grand Marnier

Dissolve sugar in milk and allow to simmer gently until the mixture thickens slightly. Melt butter in a saucepan, then add flour, mix well, add milk gradually, cook gently, stirring constantly, until a thick creamy consistency is obtained. Remove from heat, add Grand Marnier, then the yolks. Beat well. Beat whites until very stiff, fold them gently into the mixture. Pour into buttered soufflé dish, put in a moderately hot oven 233°C (450°F or Gas Mark 7) and cook for 16–18 minutes. Serve immediately.

You can vary the two recipes above using any liqueur you like.

LEMON SOUFFLÉ

4 Servings

8 sugar lumps	pinch of salt
1 large juicy lemon	2 egg yolks
6 tablespoons hot milk	4 teaspoons finely chopped
1 heaped tablespoon flour	candied orange peel (p. 205)
2 tablespoons butter	2 egg whites, beaten stiff

Rub the sugar lumps hard against the outside of a lemon to flavour them. Dissolve sugar in milk. Peel the lemon and chop rind finely.

Put the flour in a small saucepan and stir in the milk with a wooden spoon until smooth. Put the pan over low heat and add butter, stirring constantly. Simmer until smooth, add salt and remove from heat.

Beat in egg yolks, one at a time. Add lemon, candied orange and finally fold in stiffly beaten egg whites. Pour into a well-buttered soufflé dish. Bake in the oven pre-heated to 175°C (350°F or Gas Mark 3) for 25–30 minutes. Serve at once.

CHESTNUT SOUFFLÉ

4 Servings

120 grs (4 oz or ½ cup) butter	375 grs (¾ pint or 1½ cups)
3 tablespoons vanilla sugar (p. 113)	chestnut purée (p. 24)
6 beaten egg yolks	6 stiffly beaten egg whites

Mix butter (reserving a tablespoonful) with vanilla sugar and yolks, stir in chestnut purée, blend well and fold in egg whites. Pour the mixture into a buttered soufflé dish and bake in a hot oven 218°C (425°F or Gas Mark 6) for 40–45 minutes.

Serve with sour cream.

MONTELIMAR SOUFFLÉ

Infuse 120–180 grs (4–6 oz or $\frac{1}{2}$–$\frac{3}{4}$ cup) pounded nougat in the milk intended for the soufflé mixture. Prepare soufflé mixture as described in recipe for Grand Marnier Soufflé (p. 139).

Cook in the usual way.

SOUFFLÉ A LA CAMARGO

For this two layer super dessert you need two soufflé mixtures : a tangerine one (follow recipe for Orange Soufflé (p. 143) and substitute equivalent amount of tangerines for oranges) and Montelimar Soufflé mixtures (see above).

Pour the tangerine mixture into a soufflé dish, cover with sponge fingers (p. 127) sprinkled liberally with curaçao, then pour on the nougat mixture. Bake in the usual way.

Cold Soufflés

COLD ORANGE SOUFFLÉ

6 Servings

grated rind of 2 oranges
juice of 2 large oranges
juice of ½ lemon
3 egg yolks
90 grs (3 oz or 6 tablespoons)
   castor sugar

15 grs (½ oz or 2 tablespoons)
   gelatine
2 tablespoons water
1 dcl (1 gill or ½ cup) whipped
   cream
3 egg whites beaten to a stiff froth
slices of crystallized orange

Prepare soufflé dish as described in recipe for Cold Coffee Soufflé (below). Put rind into the top of a double boiler together with orange and lemon juice, stir in yolks and sugar, whisk over hot water until the mixture thickens. Dissolve gelatine in water over low heat, add to the mixture and cool. Fold in cream and egg whites, pour into soufflé dish and leave to set. Before serving remove collar and decorate with crystallised orange.

COLD COFFEE SOUFFLÉ

6 Servings

3 raw egg yolks
90 grs (3 oz or 6 tablespoons)
   castor sugar
1 dcl (1 gill or ½ cup) strong
   coffee
a few drops of vanilla essence

2–3 tablespoons sherry and 15
   grs (½ oz or 2 tablespoons)
   gelatine
1 dcl (1 gill or ½ cup) whipped
   cream
3 stiffly beaten egg whites
slices of crystallized pineapple

Extend by 7½ cm (3 inches) the height of the soufflé dish by tying around it a band of greaseproof paper, brushed with oil.

Whisk the yolks, sugar, coffee and vanilla essence in a double boiler over boiling water until the mixture thickens. Dissolve gelatine in sherry and stir into mixture. Fold in whipped cream and egg whites, pour into soufflé dish, leave to set. Remove paper, decorate with pineapple slices and serve.

CATALAN CHOCOLATE WALNUT SOUFFLÉ

6 Servings

60 grs (2 oz or 4 tablespoons) powdered unsweetened chocolate

180 grs (6 oz or 2 cups) ground walnuts

180 grs (6 oz or ¾ cup) vanilla sugar (p. 113)

4 eggs

1 teaspoon grated lemon rind

1 teaspoon butter

2½ tablespoons breadcrumbs

Pre-heat oven to 175°C (350°F or Gas Mark 3).

Mix chocolate, walnuts and sugar. Separate eggs, beat yolks and whisk into walnut mixture. Sprinkle in lemon rind and stir well. Beat egg whites into stiff peaks and fold in.

Grease a 2-litre (2-quart) soufflé dish with butter, sprinkle with breadcrumbs and turn upside down to shake off any surplus. Pour in soufflé mixture and bake for 40 minutes. Serve hot or cold.

DRAMBUIE ICED SOUFFLÉ

75 grs (2½ oz or 5 tablespoons) sugar

water

4 egg yolks

7½ grs (½ oz or 1 tablespoon) gelatine

1 glass Drambuie

4 egg whites

2½ dcl (½ pint or 1 cup) cream

3 tablespoons crushed macaroons

preserved cherries for decoration

Put sugar in a pan, add enough water to moisten, make a syrup, pour it on the yolks, stir constantly until the mixture is cold.

Dissolve gelatine in a little warm water, blend into mixture, pour in liqueur and stir well. Beat whites of egg with cream, fold into mixture. Pour into a soufflé mould with a collar of paper extending about 5 cm (2 inch) from the top. Chill. Before serving, remove paper collar, sprinkle the top with crushed macaroons and decorate with cherries.

Fruit Salads

SILVER AND GOLD FRUIT SALAD

6 Servings

2 Granny Smiths (or similar, crisp)
apples
juice of 1 lemon
1 pineapple

1 ripe grapefruit
2 oranges
3 bananas

Peel, core and slice the apples into a glass dish. Pour lemon juice over apples. Peel and core pineapple. Cut into pieces to match the apple slices and add to apples. Carefully peel grapefruit and oranges, remove the fine inner skins and pips. Orange segments can be left whole, grapefruit segments should be cut in half. Mix with the apples and pineapple. Chill. Just before serving, slice bananas and mix into the fruit salad.

SPECIAL ORANGE SALAD

8–12 Servings

12 oranges
sugar

Grand Marnier, Cointreau or
brandy

This salad is delicious and very easy to make. Choose fat, juicy, seedless oranges, if possible.

Peel the oranges, removing all the pith. Cut into very thin slices. Put a layer of orange slices into a pretty glass bowl, dredge with sugar to taste and sprinkle with Grand Marnier. Add another layer of orange slices, sugar and liqueur, until all the oranges have been used up. Chill. Before serving, spoon the juice collected at the bottom of the bowl over the oranges.

ORANGE SURPRISE

4 Servings
1 apple
2 bananas
juice of 1 lemon
4 large oranges

1 bunch seedless black grapes
2 tablespoons hazel nuts
2 tablespoons sugar
4 teaspoons brandy

Peel the apple and bananas, dice and sprinkle with lemon juice.
Cut off the top third of each orange. Scoop out the flesh of the
oranges and squeeze out juice.
Remove the grapes from the stem, add to apple and bananas.
Mix with nuts, sugar, orange juice and brandy. Fill the oranges
with the mixture. Put on the covers and chill.

ORANGE ON PINEAPPLE

6 Servings
6 slices pineapple
syrup (p. 217)

6 seedless oranges

Arrange pineapple slices on a serving dish. Boil down the syrup
until it is quite thick. Peel the rind of one orange and shred. Boil
5 minutes and drain. Peel all oranges, remove all white pith. Place
an uncooked orange on each slice of pineapple. Spoon the syrup
over each orange and sprinkle with the orange peel. Serve chilled.

JAFFA STRAWBERRY SALAD

4 Servings
750 gr (1½ lb or 4½ cups) strawberries
4 large Jaffa oranges

1 tablespoon curaçao
90 gr (3 oz or 6 tablespoons) sugar

Hull strawberries and wash quickly in cold water, without allowing them to soak. Pile in a pyramid in a serving dish. Squeeze 2
oranges and heat the juice with curaçao and sugar. As soon as
sugar dissolves and the liquid becomes syrupy, remove from heat
and while still hot pour over strawberries. Peel and slice remaining
2 oranges and garnish the dish. Serve chilled.

SPANISH ORANGE SALAD WITH POPPY SEEDS

4 Servings

4 oranges peeled
1½ tablespoon sugar
2 tablespoons orange liqueur

2 tablespoons sweet red wine
½ teaspoon poppy seeds

Cut oranges into very thin slices remove seeds, arrange slices on a serving dish. Sprinkle with sugar, liqueur and red wine and chill. Sprinkle with poppy seeds and serve.

MELON ROYAL

4–6 Servings

1 ripe melon
2 tablespoons sugar
Curaçao

brandy
Melon Granité (p. 179)

Make a circular incision around the stem of the melon. Remove the top and extract seeds. Scoop out the melon with a ball scoop, leaving only a thin shell. Sprinkle inside of melon shell with fine sugar and refrigerate.

Put scooped out melon balls into a bowl, sprinkle with sugar to taste, Curaçao and brandy, and put in refrigerator to steep for one hour.

To serve, stand the melon in a dish of crushed ice and fill with alternate layers of melon balls and melon ice. Replace the top and serve.

MELON WITH PORT OR SHERRY

Allow half a small melon per portion. Chill the melon and do not cut until nearly ready to serve. Scoop out the seeds and fibres, pour 2 tablespoons of port or sherry into the cavity, sprinkle with icing sugar and serve.

MELON SURPRISE

6–8 Servings

1 large melon
180 grs (6 oz or 1 cup) hulled
    strawberries
120 grs (4 oz or ¾ cup) raspberries

240 grs (8 oz or 1¼ cup) stoned
    cherries
1–2 sliced bananas
icing sugar
120 ml (4 oz or ½ cup) white wine

147

Cut off the top of melon, discard seeds and fibres and scoop out the flesh with a ball scoop. Turn melon upside down to drain and chill. Mix melon balls with the rest of the fruit, sprinkle with sugar to taste. Pile the fruit into the melon shell, pour wine over it, chill for 1 hour and serve.

PEACHES WITH WILD STRAWBERRIES

4 Servings

2 large peaches   icing sugar
punnet wild strawberries

Skin the peaches, cut in half, remove stones and scoop out a little of the flesh to enlarge the cavities. Fill with wild strawberries, piling them up in a mound, sprinkle with icing sugar and serve.

PINEAPPLE WITH KIRSCH

6 Servings

6 slices fresh pineapple   120 ml (¼ pint or ½ cup)
castor sugar   Kirsch

Cut away the rough outside skin and arrange pineapple slices on a serving dish. Sprinkle with sugar and leave in a cool place for 1 hour. Twenty minutes before serving, spoon Kirsch over pineapple.

RASPBERRIES ANDALOUSE

Mix raspberries with half-set redcurrant jelly (p. 214). Flavour with Maraschino.

Arrange in a mound in a fruit dish, surround the base with green figs, scored to show the pink interior. Serve with redcurrant jelly and petits fours (pp. 127–131).

SARATOGA FRUIT SALAD

6–8 Servings

1 kg (2 lbs or 4 cups) mixed diced   2 tablespoons orange flower water
or stoned fruit in season: 2–3 tablespoons Californian or
apricots, plums, apples, oranges,   other brandy
melon, grapes, cherries, peaches,   ¼ litre (½ pint or 1 cup) dry white
etc.   wine
4 tablespoons sugar

Combine all fruit in a fruit bowl, sprinkle with sugar, orange flower water and brandy. Add wine, stir, cover and chill for several hours before serving.

SHERRIED ORANGE AND GRAPE SALAD

6 Servings

6 peeled sliced oranges	4 tablespoons dry sherry
500 grs (1 lb) seedless grapes	whipped cream (p. 189) or sour
3 tablespoons sugar	cream
4 tablespoons cream sherry	

Combine orange slices and grapes in a fruit bowl. Sprinkle with sugar and the two kinds of sherry. Refrigerate 3–4 hours.
Serve with whipped cream or sour cream.

AVOCADO SALAD WITH COFFEE CREAM

4 Servings

2–3 tablespoons cream cheese	pinch ground cinnamon
1–2 tablespoons sugar	2 dcl (2 gills or 1 cup) whipped
2 tablespoons grated coconut	cream
2 avocado pears	strong black coffee
1–2 sliced bananas	

Mash the cream cheese, sweeten with half the sugar, shape into small balls, roll in coconut. Stone the avocados and scoop out flesh with a ball scoop. Arrange cream cheese and avocado balls in a glass dish with bananas, sprinkle with rest of sugar and cinnamon and chill. Before serving, flavour whipped cream with freshly made strong black coffee (cold) to taste, about 1 to 2 tablespoons. Mask the salad with it and serve.

IRAQI DRIED FRUIT AND NUT SALAD

6 Servings

180 grs (6 oz or ¾ cup) prunes	4 tablespoons sugar
180 grs (6 oz or 1 cup) dried apricots	60 grs (2 oz or 5 tablespoons) blanched peeled almonds
120 grs (4 oz or 1¼ cup) dried apple slices	3 tablespoons shelled pine kernels
1 dozen dried figs	3 tablespoons rose water
60 grs (2 oz or 6 tablespoons) seedless raisins	chipped ice

149

Wash all dried fruit, put in a bowl, cover with water and leave to soak overnight. The fruit should be cold and can therefore be left in a refrigerator.

Strain and put the liquid in which the fruit was soaked into a pan with sugar. Heat gently, stir to dissolve sugar, cook until the liquid boils down and becomes syrupy. Remove, allow to cool and chill.

Put fruit in a dish, add almonds and pine kernels, pour syrup and rose water over them, stir in crushed ice and serve.

Compôtes

APRICOT COMPÔTE

6 Servings

12 ripe apricots
180 grs (6 oz or ¾ cup) sugar
400 ml (14 oz or 1¾ cups) water

1 vanilla bean
1 tablespoon Kirsch

Plunge apricots for a second into boiling water, peel, cut in half and remove pits, reserving four of them. Put apricots into a syrup made of the sugar and water and flavoured with vanilla. Break four of the pits, divide the kernels in half, and add to the syrup. Bring to a boil gently and poach for 7–8 minutes. Do not overcook. Keep in the syrup until ready to serve. When the syrup is just warm, flavour with Kirsch and arrange on a dish. Decorate with the halved kernels, and pour the cooking syrup over them.

CHERRIES AND GOOSEBERRIES IN RED WINE

4 Servings

½ kg (1 lb or 2½ cups) stoned cherries
120 grs (4 oz or 1¼ cups) ripe gooseberries
240 grs (8 oz or 1 cup) castor sugar

360 ml (¾ pint or 1½ cups) red wine
120 ml (¼ pint or ½ cup) water
1 dozen sponge fingers (p. 127)

Mix all ingredients in a large bowl. Stand over a pan of simmering water, cover and cook for 15 minutes. Cool, chill and serve with sponge fingers.

151

BURGUNDY PEARS

6 Servings
  1 kg (2 lb) small pears
  360 grs (12 oz or 1½ cups) sugar
  120 ml (¼ pint or ½ cup) water

  1 teaspoon cinnamon
  ¼ litre (½ pint or 1 cup) red Burgundy

Peel the pears but keep them whole. Put in a saucepan with the sugar, water and cinnamon, cover and simmer for 15 minutes. Add wine and simmer 15 minutes without a cover.

Put pears in a shallow serving dish. Boil down the juice until it has the consistency of a light syrup. Pour syrup over the pears, cool and chill. Serve very cold.

HONEYED BAKED PEARS

6 Servings
  12 pears
  12 cloves
  4 tablespoons honey

  4 tablespoons lemon juice
  2 tablespoons melted butter

Peel, halve and core pears. Arrange round side up, in a shallow buttered ovenproof dish. Stick a clove into each pear. Mix honey, lemon juice and melted butter and pour over fruit. Bake for 15 minutes at 190°C (375°F or Gas Mark 4). Serve hot.

Alternatively, arrange the pears cut side up. When cooked allow to cool and fill each hollow with anything that takes your fancy: whipped cream, a candied strawberry, chopped nuts, a spoonful of brandy.

HONEYED BAKED PEACHES

As above, substituting peeled, stoned peaches for pears.

BOHEMIAN PEARS

Poach peeled, cored and halved pears in syrup, cool, arrange on a foundation of vanilla ice cream (p. 165), garnish with broken marrons glacés (p. 206), sprinkle with rum and serve.

PEACHES IN SYRUP

6 Servings

Skin 6 ripe peaches and plunge into sugar and water syrup (p. 217). Poach gently for 5 minutes. Put peaches into a glass bowl, pour syrup over them, allow to cool, sprinkle with 2 tablespoons Kirsch or Maraschino and chill for one hour.

PEACH SULTANA

Poach peaches as described in recipe for Peaches in Syrup and chill. Line a sundae dish with pistachio ice cream, (p. 165) drain the fruit, pit carefully, and place on top of ice cream.

Cover the peaches with reduced poaching syrup, chilled and flavoured with rose water.

PEACHES AURORE

Allowing one peeled peach per person, poach in syrup flavoured with Kirsch, arrange in a dessert dish on a foundation of strawberry mousse (p. 63), cover with zabaione (p. 65) and serve.

CARDINAL PEACHES

Allowing one peeled peach per person, poach in syrup, serve on a foundation of raspberry purée, flavoured with Kirsch or Maraschino, sprinkle the top with slivered almonds and serve.

STRAWBERRIES ROMANOFF

Put hulled strawberries in a fruit bowl, moisten with orange juice, sprinkle with curaçao and serve with crème chantilly (p. 189).

STRAWBERRIES IN CHAMPAGNE

This is a delicious and not filling dessert, strictly for extra festive occasions and guaranteed to go to your head.

It is a popular dessert among Californian winemaking families. The expert who runs one of the wineries we visited advocated rinsing the strawberries by merely dipping them in a cup of dry white wine, because 'water dilutes the flavour'.

4–6 Servings

1 kg (2 lb or 1 quart) hulled strawberries	3–4 tablespoons sugar
2–3 tablespoons brandy	bottle iced Brut Champagne

Slice large strawberries, leave small ones whole. Put them into a glass bowl, sprinkle with brandy and chill. When ready to take the fruit to the table, sprinkle with sugar. At the table, pour some champagne over the strawberries and serve at once while the champagne is still bubbling. Drink the rest of the champagne with the dessert.

STRAWBERRIES IN SYRUP

6 Servings

Bring ¼ litre (½ pint or 1 cup) water and 5 tablespoons sugar to a boil. Add 1 litre (1 quart) washed, hulled strawberries and return to a boil. Remove from heat. Chill. Serve over cake with whipped cream, or with vanilla ice cream. Flavour with Kirsch if desired.

CHERRIES IN SYRUP

Choose ripe cherries, stem, wash and remove pits. Proceed as for strawberries in syrup.

CHERRIES IN BRANDY

Use ripe, unstoned cherries and leave stalks on.
Proceed as for Strawberries in Syrup, but add 1 clove and a piece of cinnamon to sugar and water. Remove from heat and while still warm, add brandy to taste.

SABRA DESSERT / PRICKLY PEAR COMPÔTE

This is an Israeli national dessert. The Hebrew word for prickly pear is sabra and this is the name which the children of the one time immigrants, native Israelis, have adopted. Thus an Israeli born girl is called sabra, because like her name-sake, the fruit of the cactus, she is 'prickly on the outside and sweet inside'.

4 Servings

8 prickly pears	⅔ litres (14 oz or 1¾ cups) water
120 grs (4 oz or ½ cup) sugar	1 tablespoon lemon juice

Peel the prickly pears and leave them whole.

Heat sugar with water, slowly bring to the boil, simmer for 5 minutes.

Add prickly pears, cook for 2–3 minutes and remove from heat. Sprinkle in lemon juice. Serve hot or cold.

SUMMER COMPÔTE

6 Servings

½ kg (1 lb) black cherries	250 grs (½ lb) redcurrants
½ kg (1 lb) dessert gooseberries	sugar
250 grs (½ lb) raspberries	whipped cream (p. 189)

Wash all the fruit. Stone the cherries, top and tail the gooseberries and redcurrants, hull the raspberries. Heat the cherries, gooseberries and redcurrants gently in a saucepan for 5 minutes. Add raspberries and sugar to taste. Cook gently for a further 5 minutes.

Serve hot or cold, with whipped cream.

Jellies

LEMON EGG JELLY

3-4 Servings

2 lemons
180 grs (6 oz or ¾ cup) sugar
water

15 grs (½ oz or 2 tablespoons) gelatine
2 eggs

Wipe the lemons, peel them thinly, put the peel into a saucepan with the sugar, the juice of 2 lemons and enough water to make ½ litre (1 pint or 2 cups) liquid. Simmer for 10 minutes. Dilute gelatine in 120 ml (4 oz or ½ cup) water, stir to dissolve completely and blend into lemon mixture. Stir well, remove from heat and allow to cool.

Break the eggs into a bowl, whisk, strain the mixture on to the eggs, return to saucepan, cook gently until it thickens, without allowing it to boil. Cool and pour into a mould, rinsed out with cold water. Chill to set.

CRIMEAN LEMON JELLY WITH GRAPES

6 Servings

240 grs (8 oz) loaf sugar
rind of 2 lemons
1 litre (1 quart) water
60 grs (2 oz or ½ cup) gelatine
240 ml (½ pint or 1 cup) lemon juice

1 stick cinnamon
4 tablespoons white wine (or sherry)
whites of 2 eggs
washed shells of 2 eggs
½ kg (1 lb) grapes

Put sugar, lemon rind and all but ½ cup of water into a saucepan, heat gently to boiling point, leave to simmer for 3-4 minutes. Dissolve gelatine in reserved water. Add lemon juice, cinnamon and gelatine to sugar and water syrup and stir well. Add wine. Beat the egg whites stiff, crush egg shells and add both to the liquid jelly. (The egg whites and shells will clarify the jelly.) Whisk the mixture over low heat until it comes to the boil, remove and allow to settle for a couple of minutes. Boil up once again, whisking vigorously, remove from heat and rest as before. Repeat whisking and boiling up for the third time, remove from heat, leave to stand for a few minutes and strain through a jelly bag.

Peel the grapes, if the skins are tough, and remove pips. Coat a rinsed mould with a thin layer of jelly, refrigerate until this lining is half set, put in a layer of grapes and spoon in a little jelly to set them. Continue in this way until all grapes and jelly are used up. If you have enough grapes only to put in a layer or two, fill up with lemon jelly, but make sure it is cool before you pour it into the mould. Chill until set.

ORANGE BLOSSOM JELLY

4 Servings

15 grs (½ oz or 2 tablespoons) gelatine
juice of one lemon
120 grs (4 oz or ½ cup) sugar
¼ litre (½ pint or 1 cup) hot water

120 ml (4 oz or ½ cup) dry white wine
4 tablespoons double strength orange blossom water
1 stiffly beaten egg white
1 crushed egg shell

Dissolve gelatine in lemon juice. Bring sugar gently to the boil with water and white wine, stir until dissolved. Add orange blossom water. Clarify with egg white and shell as described above. Strain through a jelly bag, pour into a rinsed mould and leave to set.

RASPBERRY KISEL

Kisel is a very popular Russian sweet, usually made of fresh berries, very smooth and velvety. It is served with double cream and can be eaten hot or cold. No gelatine is used in its preparation; the texture is achieved by adding various amounts of cornflour or potato flour.

There are three recognised consistencies: fairly stiff, if kisel is to be served cold and turned out of the mould; semi-stiff if it is to be served hot; and liquid when it is intended as a dessert sauce.

With cold kisel, the cream is served separately. When kisel is served hot, the cream is stirred into it.

4–6 Servings

½ kg (1 lb or 3 cups) raspberries
½ litre (1 pint or 2 cups) water
120 grs (4 oz or ½ cup) sugar

2 tablespoons cornflour
cream

Bring berries to the boil with water, simmer for 20–25 minutes and strain through a muslin bag, but do not press too hard, as this might cause clouding. Reserve 3 tablespoons of this raspberry juice. Return the rest to pan, add sugar, gently bring to the boil, simmer, stirring until sugar dissolves completely. Mix cornflour with re-served raspberry juice and blend into the pan. Simmer, stirring constantly until the kisel thickens. Remove from heat, pour into a rinsed mould, cool and chill. Serve with cream.

Strawberries, gooseberries, blackcurrants all make excellent kisels. Kissel sauces are excellent with rice desserts.

ROSE PETAL JELLY

6 Servings

lemon jelly
360 grs (12 oz or 1 cup) rose petal jam (p. 213)
2 egg whites beaten stiff

2 crushed egg shells
2 tablespoons triple strength rose water

Prepare lemon jelly (p. 157). Add rose petal jam, clarify with egg white and shells, as described, add rose water and strain, pour into mould and chill.

TANGERINE BASKETS

This is a traditional Japanese Girls' Festival dessert and a delicious way of serving tangerines.

4 Servings

4 tangerines
4 leaves gelatine

¼ litre (½ pint or 1 cup) water
120 grs (4 oz or ½ cup) sugar

Cut each tangerine to make it look like a small basket with a handle on top. To do this, hold the tangerine stalk end up, make two parallel cuts 1¼ cm (½ inch) apart (less, if you want a more slender handle, though they tend to be rather fragile), on both sides of the top centre down to a third of the fruit from the top. Then cut horizontally on each side of the handle and remove the two pieces cut out. Carefully extract the pulp and squeeze out its juice into a small bowl. You should now have a small-handled basket. Repeat the procedure for the rest of the tangerines. Melt gelatine in water, add sugar and tangerine juice, leave until jelly begins to set, spoon into tangerine baskets and chill.

MINT AND MELON JELLY

4 Servings

1 honey dew melon
120 grs (4 oz or ½ cup) sugar
4 tablespoons fresh chopped mint
30 grs (1 oz) gelatine

4 tablespoons lemon juice
1–2 tablespoons Crème de Menthe
4–5 ice cubes
mint leaves for garnish

Cut melon, discard seeds and scoop out the flesh with a ball scoop. Keep the juice which comes out of the melon. Put sugar in a pan with 240 ml (8 oz or 1 cup) water, heat, gently, bring to the boil, simmer syrup for 5–6 minutes. Put chopped mint in a bowl, pour hot syrup over it and leave to infuse. When the minty syrup is cold, strain.

Dissolve gelatine in 180 ml (6 oz or ¾ cup) cold water and stir into syrup. Add lemon juice and Crème de Menthe, to intensify colour. Add ice cubes and stir until they melt and cool down the mixture. Reserve a dozen melon balls for garnishing, add the rest, together with any melon juice to the jelly liquid. Rinse a mould with cold water, pour the mixture into it and chill to set.

To serve, turn out, garnish with mint leaves and melon balls. The melon shell makes a good container for Orange and Lemon Sorbet (p. 171).

BLUE MOUNTAIN RUM JELLY

6–8 Servings

2 tablespoons gelatine
120 ml (¼ pint or ½ cup) cold
   water

¾ litre (1½ pints or 3 cups) strong
   hot coffee
2 tablespoons jamaica rum
120 grs (4 oz or ½ cup) sugar

Soak gelatine in cold water for 5 minutes. Add hot coffee and rum and stir until gelatine is dissolved. Add sugar and stir well. Pour into individual glasses. Chill until firm. The jelly can also be poured into a mould, chilled and unmoulded before serving with rum flavoured whipped cream.

SHERRIED EGG JELLY

This makes an excellent and delicious pick-me-up.

1–2 Servings

juice and rind of 1 lime (or
   lemon)
1–2 tablespoons sherry
cold water

6 tablespoons sugar
1 tablespoon powdered gelatine
1 egg

Mix lime juice, rind and sherry and add enough water to make up liquid to 2½ dcl (½ pint or 1 cup). Pour into a pan, add sugar and gelatine, stir and heat gently to dissolve, but do not allow to boil. Cover, leave to infuse the lime rind for 10 minutes, strain, stir in lightly beaten egg, heat over a pan of water gently to thicken the mixture, stirring constantly. Pour into a mould rinsed with cold water and chill until set.

CHAMPAGNE JELLY

8–10 Servings

30 grs (1 oz or 4 tablespoons) plain gelatine
120 ml (4 oz or ½ cup) strawberry wine
120 grs (4 oz or ½ cup) sugar
⅛ teaspoon salt

½ litre (1 pint or 2 cups) hot water
360 ml (12 oz or 1½ cups) chilled champagne
whipped cream (p. 189)
8–10 fresh strawberries

Soften gelatine in strawberry wine. Add sugar, salt and hot water. Stir until sugar and gelatine are completely dissolved. Cool, chill until the mixture turns syrupy, then whisk champagne into it. Pour into serving glasses and chill until the jelly sets. Pipe or spoon a topping of whipped cream on the jelly, decorate each with a beautiful strawberry and serve.

Ice Creams

BASIC PREPARATION

ICE CREAMS

Delicious ice creams, based on eggs, sugar syrup, cream or milk and fruit, can quite easily be made at home. If you are lucky enough to have a churn type freezer, you can produce ices of perfect creamy texture, but even if you have no other freezing equipment than your ice trays, you can still produce home-made ice creams far superior to any ready-made concoction.

If using a churn freezer, pour the ice cream mixture (which should be cold) into the metal freezer container, lodged in a bucket packed with layers of chipped ice and salt, allowing 1 part of salt to 6 of ice. Do not fill the churn more than two-thirds full, to allow for expansion. Turn the handle with a regular rhythm, stir the ice cream mixture from time to time, carefully replacing the lid each time to avoid salt getting into the mixture. Add more chipped ice and salt as the packing melts.

If using ice trays, switch your refrigerator to the coldest setting 30–40 minutes before you plan to start freezing your mixture. The rest of your supplies will not suffer from this, but please remember to re-set indicator to normal position when the ice cream is ready. Allow the mixture to thicken, which takes about 30–40 minutes, depending on how quickly your refrigerator works, then beat the mixture and return to freezer. This beating is essential; by whisking air into the mixture, you ensure lightness of texture. Continue to freeze until the ice cream is firm – anything from 40–60 minutes. Do not overfreeze – if you make it brick-like in texture, it will be about as much pleasure to eat.

Whichever method of freezing you adopt, there are three important points to bear in mind for successful ice cream making:

(1) Make sure the mixture is cold before pouring into freezing containers.

(2) Use icing sugar whenever possible, for smoother texture.

(3) Taste the mixture for sweetness.

It should be pleasantly sweet. If you put in too much sugar, the ice will not freeze; if not enough, it will be like a rock.

Also bear in mind that both sweetness and flavourings are absorbed by freezing – don't cut down the quantities given in the recipes.

CUSTARDS FOR ICE CREAMS

Custards for ice creams can be made with cream, milk or a mixture of both. Expense is the only consideration, although whatever you save on cream and milk, will be offset by having to use more eggs. The three recipes given below have all been tried out and proved successful for freezing in refrigerator ice trays.

ICE CREAM CUSTARD

6 Servings

360 ml (12 oz or 1½ cups) very fresh cream	4 yolks
flavouring (vanilla bean, thinly cut lemon or orange peel, etc.)	120 grs (4 oz or 8 tablespoons) icing sugar (or pounded castor sugar)

Put cream and flavouring into a double boiler, stir in yolks, heat, stirring all the time over simmering water until the mixture thickens. Remove from heat but continue to stir for a few minutes. Add sugar, stir to dissolve and blend in, allow to cool, strain and use as required.

HALF AND HALF ICE CREAM CUSTARD

¼ litre (½ pint or 1 cup) milk ¼ litre (½ pint or 1 cup) single cream 6 yolks	thinly sliced lemon peel, without pith 90–120 grs (3–4 oz or 7–8 tablespoons) sugar

Using above ingredients, proceed as described in recipe for Ice Cream Custard (see above).

VANILLA ICE CREAM, SPANISH STYLE

6 yolks
¾ litre (1½ pints or 3 cups) milk
1 teaspoon vanilla
pinch salt

300 grs (10 oz or 1¼ cups) sugar
2½ dcl (½ pint or 1 cup) whipped
cream

Beat the yolks and dilute with a little milk. Scald the rest of the milk with vanilla, salt and sugar and heat to dissolve stirring all the time. Remove from heat, one by one stir in yolks, pour mixture into a double saucepan, cook until the mixture thickens over simmering water (8–10 minutes), stirring constantly. When the mixture coats the back of a wooden spoon, remove from heat (i.e. take the pan with the custard mixture out of hot water), stir to cool. Strain, add whipped cream and freeze.

ALMOND ICE CREAM

Make vanilla ice cream mixture (above), add 120 grs (4 oz or ⅔ cup) almonds and 4 bitter almonds, blanched and pounded with 2–3 tablespoons water. Mix well and freeze.

HAZEL NUT OR PISTACHIO ICE CREAM

As Almond Ice Cream, substituting 180 grs (6 oz or 1 cup) blanched and pounded hazel nuts or pistachio nuts for almonds.

WALNUT ICE CREAM

Vanilla, coffee or chocolate ice cream, (see recipes), 150 grs (5 oz or 1⅔ cups) peeled ground walnuts. Prepare ice cream, adding the walnuts with the whipped cream.

STRAWBERRY OR RASPBERRY ICE CREAM

Prepare ice cream custard as described and add the sieved pulp from ½ kg (1 lb or 2 cups) of fresh strawberries or raspberries and proceed as described.

(Red currants and other soft fruit can also be used for ice creams.)

COFFEE ICE CREAM

Add 120 grs (4 oz or 9 tablespoons) freshly roasted coffee beans to the uncooked custard mixture (p. 164). Cook as described. When the custard thickens to the desired consistency, remove from heat and leave to infuse for 2–3 hours. Strain and freeze as described.

CHOCOLATE ICE CREAM

Dissolve 180 grs (6 oz or 1½ cups) grated chocolate in the milk intended for ice cream custard (see Vanilla Ice Cream, Spanish Style). Make the custard as usual and freeze.

MANGO ICE CREAM

6–8 Servings

3 egg yolks
360 ml (12 oz or 1½ cups) milk
1 teaspoon vanilla essence
¼ teaspoon salt
100 grs (3½ oz or 7 tablespoons) sugar

240 grs (8 oz) fresh or tinned mangoes
240 ml (½ pint or 1 cup) whipped cream

Beat the yolks and dissolve in a small quantity of milk. Scald the rest of the milk with vanilla, salt and sugar, simmer gently until the sugar is completely dissolved. Remove from heat, blend gradually with yolks, pour into a double saucepan, cook over simmering water for a few minutes until the mixture thickens enough to coat the spoon. Remove, continue to stir while the mixture cools, strain and chill but do not allow to freeze hard. Slice mangoes, stir into mixture, fold in whipped cream and chill until ready to serve.

TANGERINE ICE CREAM

300 grs (10 oz or 1¼ cup) sugar
1 dcl (1 gill or ½ cup) water
peel of 3 tangerines
juice of 6 tangerines

juice of 2 oranges
juice of 1 lemon
3 yolks
3 eggs

Boil sugar with water to make a syrup. When the syrup begins to form a thread* add tangerine, orange and lemon juice. Beat the yolks and the eggs together and pour them on the syrup. Cook in a double saucepan, stirring constantly until the mixture thickens. Strain, cool and freeze in the usual way.

APRICOT ICE CREAM

½ kg (1 lb) apricots   ¼ litre (½ pint or 1 cup) cream
125 grs (4 oz or ½ cup) sugar   4 yolks

Choose ripe apricots, scald in boiling water, stone and reduce to a purée.

Prepare ice cream custard, using sugar, cream and yolks as described (p. 164). Add apricot purée, mix well and freeze.

PEACH ICE CREAM

Follow instructions for Apricot Ice Cream

PRALINE ICE CREAM

Add to 1 litre (1 quart) Vanilla Ice Cream (p. 165) 120 grs (4 oz or ½ cup) praline (p. 218) pounded and rubbed through a sieve. (Burnt hazelnuts, pistachio nuts or peanuts may also be used.)

STREGA ICE CREAM

Prepare half and half ice cream custard (p. 164). When adding whipped cream, incorporate in the mixture 6 tablespoons of Strega, freeze as described.

Other liqueurs can be used for flavouring ice cream mixtures. Grand Marnier, Maraschino, Kirsch are particularly recommended.

* Note: This is the first stage in the cooking of sugar. It has a density of 25° and registers 102°C (215°F) on the Baumé thermometer (saccharometer). If you don't use a thermometer, test by dipping the tip of a finger and thumb into cold water, then into syrup and back into cold water. Press finger and thumb together and separate them slowly to check if a fine thread is formed.

167

COINTREAU (GRAND MARNIER, MARASCHINO OR KIRSCH) ICE CREAM

Prepare half and half ice cream custard (p. 164). When adding whipped cream, incorporate in the mixture 6 tablespoons of Cointreau, freeze as described.

Other liqueurs can be used for flavouring ice cream mixtures. Grand Marnier, Maraschino, Kirsch are particularly recommended.

MARASHINO-FLAVOURED CHESTNUT ICE CREAM

Combine equal quantities of ice cream custard and sieved chestnut purée. Freeze until the mixture thickens. Beat in whipped cream and 2–3 tablespoons maraschino. Finish freezing. For proportion of ingredients see Ice Cream Custards (pp. 164–5).

JASMINE TEA ICE CREAM

2 teaspoons China jasmine tea	¾ litre (1½ pints or 3 cups) scalded milk
1 dcl (1 gill or ½ cup) boiling water	4 yolks
	240 grs (8 oz or 1 cup) sugar

Pour water on the tea, cover and allow to stand. Strain, mix with milk and add to yolks creamed with sugar. Blend, simmer in a double saucepan until the mixture thickens, strain, cool and freeze.

MARBLE ICE CREAM

Prepare and freeze in one container either Vanilla Ice Cream, or Orange Blossom Ice Cream, and in another container Strawberry or Raspberry Ice Cream. When both are ready, mix to give the ice cream a marble effect, re-chill and serve.

LEMON FLAVOURED MERINGUE ICE CREAM

Ice Cream Custard (pp. 164–5)	4 whites of egg, beaten into a stiff froth
lemon juice to taste	powdered cinnamon

Prepare ice cream custard flavoured with lemon juice and put in the freezer. When nearly frozen, fold in whites of egg and complete freezing. Serve sprinkled with cinnamon.

Sherbets, Water Ices

JAFFA ICE

6 Servings

6 large Jaffa oranges	240 grs (8 oz or 1 cup) sugar

Slice off top of the oranges, scoop out all pulp. Press out and keep the juice and the shells.

Put sugar to heat with 2 tablespoons water and simmer the syrup until it reaches thread degree. Test by tapping with a spoon. If the syrup forms a fibrous thread, it is ready. If you use a sugar thermometer, this degree is reached at 105°C (220°F). Remove pan from heat and add orange juice. Return to heat and cook until the syrup reaches thread degree once more. Freeze in ice cream freezer.

Tidy up the orange shells, carefully cutting away filaments. Fill with iced mixture, chill and serve.

PINEAPPLE ICE

4–6 Servings

½ litre (1 pint or 2 cups) syrup (p. 217)	Kirsch
180 grs (6 oz or ½ cup) shredded pineapple	Maraschino

Cook syrup as described, mix with pineapple, flavour to taste with Kirsch and Maraschino and freeze.

FROSTY GRAPEFRUIT

6 Servings

3 grapefruit	240 grs (8 oz or 1 cup) sugar

Cut each grapefruit in half. Scoop out and press out the juice. Keep the shells.

Add 2 tablespoons of water to the sugar and cook until it reaches thread degree (p. 167). Remove from heat and add grapefruit juice. Re-heat until it starts to form a thread. Freeze the mixture in an ice cream freezer. Fill the grapefruit shells with the mixture and chill.

CONNECTICUT CRANBERRY SHERBET

6 Servings
½ kg (1 lb or 2 cups) cranberries   180 grs (6 oz or ½ cup) clear
1 litre (1 quart) sweet cider   honey
                                     a sprig of mint

Simmer the cranberries in cider and cool. Blend all ingredients until smooth. Turn into an ice-tray and freeze until mushy. Beat thoroughly and put back in freezer to finish freezing.

LIQUEUR SHERBET

8 Servings
½ kg (1 lb or 2 cups) sugar   120 ml (¼ pint or ½ cup) fruit
1 litre (2 quarts) water   liqueur (blackcurrant, apricot,
                                   cherry, etc.)

Bring sugar and water gently to the boil, stir to dissolve, cook for 5 minutes. Cool, add liqueur, pour into a freezer tray and freeze. From time to time scrape the sides of the tray to detach any sherbet sticking to them, but don't stir this scraped-off sherbet into the rest of the mixture. When properly frozen, sherbet should have a slightly gritty texture.

Remove from freezer with a conical sherbet scoop. Set each portion point upwards in a sherbet cup and serve with a sprinkling of the same liqueur. If you have no conical scoop, shape the sherbet to a point with a spoon.

WINE SHERBET

8 Servings
½ kg (1 lb or 2 cups) sugar   juice of 2 lemons
½ litre (1 pint or 2 cups) water   juice of 1 orange
250 ml (½ pint or 1 cup) Sauternes

Sauternes, port, Madeira and Champagne all make excellent sherbets. Follow recipe for Liqueur Sherbet.

Make syrup using sugar, water and wine. Cook for 5 minutes,

add lemon and orange juice, pour into freezer tray, cool and freeze. From time to time scrape sherbet off the sides of the tray, as described.

BOSTON BUTTERMILK SHERBET

6 Servings

4 tablespoons honey
180 grs (6 oz or ¾ cup) any fruit purée. (Use sieved fresh soft fruits, or cooked apple or apricot purée.)

360 ml (¾ pint or 1½ cups) buttermilk
zest of 1 lemon
2 egg whites

Blend honey and fruit purée. Add buttermilk, lemon juice and rind. Pour into a refrigerator tray and freeze until firm. Turn into a bowl and beat well. Whisk the egg whites to stiff peaks and fold into the mixture. Freeze again and serve.

ORANGE AND LEMON SORBET IN MELON SHELL

4 Servings

1 melon shell
500 grs (1 lb or 2 cups) sugar
180 ml (6 oz or ¾ cup) water

juice of 2 oranges and 2 lemons
2 egg whites

Save the melon shell when using the flesh for a fruit salad or other dessert (see recipe for Mint and Melon Jelly (p. 160). Cut the top of the melon, remove seeds with a spoon, then carefully scoop out flesh without damaging the shell. Keep the shell in refrigerator. Boil sugar with water to make syrup. Add orange and lemon juice. Cool, chill in ice tray in refrigerator. When the mixture is almost set, stir it, put back in refrigerator and leave until it begins to thicken.

Beat the egg whites until stiff. Add to sorbet mixture, stir and chill until firm.

Fill the melon shells with the sorbet and keep in refrigerator until ready to serve.

AVOCADO SORBET IN LIME OR LEMON CUPS

6 Servings

juice and shells of 4 limes (or lemons)
2 avocados

small pinch salt
1 teaspoon grated lime rind
240 gr (8 oz or ⅔ cup) honey

You will only need 6 half lime shells for freezing and serving the sorbet, but an extra lime or two may be needed to make up the right amount of juice. Squeeze out the juice and strain, measuring out 120 ml (4 oz or ½ cup). Then take the squeezed halved limes, carefully pare away all pith and membranes to enlarge the cups and cut a little slice off the end of each to make them stable. Alternately, stand the lime shells in egg cups. Peel and dice the avocados, put through a blender with salt, lime juice, grated lime rind and honey. When the blended mixture is smooth, pour into refrigerator. Pile into lime cups and serve.

Bombes, Parfaits

BOMBES

12 Servings
360 grs (12 oz or 1½ cups) sugar
360 ml (12 oz or 1½ cups) water
16 egg yolks
flavouring

½ litre (1 pint or 2 cups) whipped
  cream
vanilla ice cream (p. 165)

Boil sugar and water for 5 minutes. Cool. Put syrup and egg yolks in a double boiler over low heat. Stir with a whisk, as for custard. When the mixture thickens and begins to form a ribbon, remove from heat and continue to whisk until cool. Add flavouring (extract, liqueur, purée of peaches or apricots, etc.). Fold in whipped cream.

Line a mould with frozen vanilla ice cream, then fill with the above mixture. Freeze. Unmould just before serving.

As a variation, you can line the mould with chocolate ice cream (p. 166) and fill the bombe with praline ice cream (p. 167), or invent a combination of your own.

BISCUIT TORTONI

2½ dcl (½ pint or 1 cup) double
  cream
2½ dcl (½ pint or 1 cup) single
  cream
60 grs (2 oz or 4 tablespoons)
  icing sugar

pinch salt
1 glass sweet sherry
120 grs (4 oz or 1¼ cups)
  macaroon crumbs

Whip both creams with sugar and salt. Freeze until firm. Transfer to a bowl (preferably the bowl of an electric mixer) and mix in the sherry and 1 cup of macaroon crumbs. Freeze in an oblong metal loaf tin. Unmould to serve and sprinkle with remaining macaroon crumbs. Cut in slices and serve.

The easiest way to unmould ice creams, without risking the danger of making them too runny, is to upturn the mould on to a chilled serving dish and put a cloth wrung out in very hot water round the mould for a few seconds.

ICED WALNUT GÂTEAU

6 Servings

360 grs (12 oz or 3 cups) walnuts   1 teaspoon butter
6 egg yolks   6 stiffly beaten whites of egg
300 grs (10 oz or 1¼ cups) sugar   Vanilla Custard Cream (pp. 164–5)

Grind the nuts into coarse flour, mix three quarters of it with yolks. Beat until the mixture is well blended. Add sugar and repeat beating to amalgamate the ingredients.

Pre-heat oven to 220°C (400°F or Gas Mark 5). Butter 2 layer cake tins. Fold stiffly beaten egg whites into the walnut mixture, lifting gently to keep it as light as possible. Divide the gateau mixture equally between the two tins and bake for 10 minutes. Cool before removing from tins.

Mix reserved ground walnuts with vanilla custard cream to make filling. Spread filling on one of the cakes and set the other one on top, to make a two-tier sandwich. Chill for several hours before serving.

PARFAITS

Originally the parfait was an iced sweet, flavoured with coffee. Now parfaits are made with many kinds of flavouring.

360 grs (12 oz or 1½ cups) sugar   ½ litre (1 pint or 2 cups) whipped
360 ml (12 oz or 1½ cups) water   cream
16 egg yolks   flavouring

Proceed as for bombes (p. 173) using one of the flavourings listed below. Freeze the mixture in a parfait mould. Flavourings recommended for parfaits : coffee, chocolate, vanilla, ground almonds, hazel nuts, pistachio nuts, walnuts, praline, puréed oranges, lemons, redcurrants, raspberries, strawberries, cherries, apricots (when sweet fruit is used, a few tablespoons of orange or lemon juice heighten the flavour), banana, pineapple, melon, crystallized violets and rose petals, Maraschino, Benedictine, Grand Marnier, Pernod, Cointreau, Chartreuse rum, Kirsch, etc.

Coupes, Sundaes

COUPES / SUNDAES

Coupes or sundaes are composite sweets with ice cream as principal ingredient. In France originally they were served in champagne glasses or silver ice cups, which accounts for their name. Now the American tradition of serving them in tall glasses is more popular.

Fill the glasses with several kinds of ice cream, decorate with fresh or crystallised fruit and top with whipped cream.

COUPE JACQUES

This along with Pêche Melba, is the best known of classical French iced coupes. Many other variations can be made using this recipe as a model and varying the ingredients.

peeled diced peaches	crystallised cherries or fresh
Kirsch and/or Maraschino	strawberries
lemon ice (p. 171)	halved fresh almonds
strawberry ice (p. 165)	

Sprinkle peaches with kirsch or maraschino, or mixture of both. Leave to steep. Fill ice cups with alternate scoops of lemon and strawberry ice cream, put a tablespoon of diced peach in the middle. Decorate with cherries or strawberries, spike with halved almonds, sprinkle with a little Kirsch or Maraschino and serve.

COUPE HÉLÈNE

Fill ice cups with vanilla ice cream (p. 165), decorate with a circle of pralined violets, add a whorl of Crème Chantilly (p. 189) in the middle and sprinkle with grated chocolate.

Pralined violets are obtainable from good confectioners. We buy crystallised violets and dip them in praline (p. 218).

BANANA COUPE

Put sliced bananas sprinkled with Curaçao in the bottom of ice cups and fill with orange ice (pp. 171 and 179).

PINEAPPLE COUPE WITH MERINGUES

6–8 Servings

1 shredded pineapple
Kirsh and/or Maraschino
vanilla ice cream (p. 165)
12–16 small meringue shells
  (p. 95)

pineapple ice (p. 169)
240 grs (8 oz or 1¼ cups) fresh
  strawberry purée
Crème Chantilly (p. 189)

Sprinkle pineapple with Kirsch or Maraschino or a mixture of both. Put some pineapple in each chilled ice cup. Fill half way with vanilla ice cream.

Fill meringue shells with pineapple ice cream, sandwich in pairs and put one such double filled meringue shell into each cup. Cover meringues with strawberry purée and pipe a spoonful of Chantilly around them.

PEACH MELBA

On a foundation of vanilla ice cream (p. 165) put peeled peaches, steeped in vanilla-flavoured syrup and chilled. Top with raspberry purée.

Many other kinds of fruit may be served in the same way: large strawberries sprinkled with sugar or Kirsch; pears or nectarines, treated as peaches above, etc.

ICE CREAM WITH PEACHES

6–8 Servings

1 kg (2 lb) ripe peaches
270 grs (9 oz or 1 cup plus 2
  tablespoons) sugar
2 tablespoons brandy
4 yolks

¾ litre (1½ pints or 3 cups) milk
water
90 grs (3 oz or 1 cup) ground
  almonds

Peel, stone and quarter the peaches. Put them in a bowl, sprinkle with 90 grs (3 oz or 6 tablespoons) sugar and brandy and leave to soak overnight in a refrigerator. Using 90 grs (3 oz or 6 tablespoons) sugar, 4 yolks and the milk, make ice cream custard (p. 164). Put 90 grs (3 oz or 6 tablespoons) sugar with just enough water to moisten it into a saucepan and prepare a caramel syrup, i.e. boil without stirring until it acquires a rich brown colour (p. 217). Add almonds, cook gently, stirring all the time until the paste turns golden. Add this paste to the ice cream mixture, blend well, cool and freeze. Serve in individual glasses, with peaches and the liquid poured over.

Granités, Marquises

REDCURRANT GRANITÉ

6–8 Servings

Extract the juice from red and white currants and press through a jelly bag. For 1 litre (1 quart) juice, dissolve ½ kg (1 lb or 2 cups) in ½ litre (1 pint or 2 cups) water. Boil for 5 minutes. Chill the syrup, add the juice, mix well and freeze.

MELON GRANITÉ

4–6 Servings

Mix ½ kg (1 lb or 2 cups) of melon pulp, rubbed through a sieve, with chilled sugar syrup—240 grs (8 oz or 1 cup) sugar and 240 ml (½ pint or 1 cup) water boiled for 5 minutes. Freeze.

ORANGE GRANITÉ

4 Servings

240 ml (½ pint or 1 cup) water   grated rind and juice of 4 oranges
240 grs (8 oz or 1 cup) sugar   juice of 1 lemon

Mix the sugar and water and infuse the rind in it. Boil for 5 minutes. Chill the syrup and add orange and lemon juice. Strain and freeze.

MARQUISES

Prepare the same as for sherbet (pp. 169–172) with fruit liqueur, but use Kirsch-flavoured pineapple juice or crushed strawberries (one part juice to one part syrup).

At the last moment blend in $\frac{1}{2}$ litre (1 pint or 2 cups) of whipped cream to 1 litre (1 quart or 4 cups) of frozen sherbet mixture. Serve in small glass goblets.

WATERMELON ICE LOLLIES

1 ripe watermelon   1 sprig of mint

Blend watermelon flesh and mint in blender (or rub through a sieve). Pour into ice-lolly moulds and put in freezer compartment of refrigerator. Insert sticks when the lollies are almost set.

This recipe is also recommended for Canteloupe melon and all soft fruits.

Dough, Pastry, Batters

SHORT PASTRY

500 grs (1 lb or 4 cups) sifted
  flour
240 grs (8 oz or 1 cup) sugar
120 grs (4 oz or ½ cup) butter

pinch salt
cold water
1 tablespoon orange blossom
  water (optional)

Combine flour, sugar, butter and salt. Rub the butter lightly
into the flour with your fingertips. Mix to a stiff paste with cold
water. Flavour with Orange blossom water and use as required.

SUGAR PASTRY

150 grs (5 oz or 10 tablespoons)
  butter
75 grs (2½ oz or 5 tablespoons)
  sugar

420 grs (14 oz or 3¼ cups) sifted
  flour
1 egg
⅛ teaspoon salt

Soften the butter over lowest possible heat and stir in the sugar
with a wooden spoon until a creamy consistency is reached. Heap
flour on a working surface. Make a well in the centre, put in egg,
sugar and butter mixture and salt. Work with your fingertips
just to blend the ingredients. The mixture is crumbly so take
care in rolling out and flour both your board and your rolling
pin throughly.

PUFF PASTRY OR FLAKY PASTRY

240 grs (½ lb or 2 cups) sifted
  flour
½ teaspoon salt

7 tablespoons cold water
1 tablespoon lemon juice
240 grs (½ lb or 1 cup) butter

Put the flour on a board in a circle, make a well in the middle,
put in salt. Combine water and lemon juice, moisten the flour

with it, and work the paste with your fingers very quickly to form a ball of fairly firm dough. Leave for 20 minutes. To make sure your butter is exactly the same consistency as the dough, knead it (either on a pastry-slab or in a lightly floured cloth) to soften to the correct degree.

Roll out the paste into a sheet to a thickness of 6 mm ($\frac{1}{4}$ inch), which should give you a strip of 15 cm by 45 cm (6 inches by 18 inches). Put the butter in the middle, fold the ends of the paste so as to enclose it completely, and leave for 10 minutes in a cold place.

Roll out the pastry on a lightly floured board, refold the strip in three, i.e. fold each end towards the middle. Leave for 10 minutes. This is called giving the pastry a turn (*tourage*) – the second turn is done by rolling out the folded paste in the opposite direction, and so forth. Give four more turns to the paste, rolling out and turning the strip each time and leaving it to rest in a cold place for 10 minutes between each turn.

The purpose of all this turning and rolling is to spread the butter evenly in the paste. In between turns, keep in a cold place, but do not allow the butter to freeze and harden, otherwise you will have trouble in getting the two elements – flour and water paste and butter – to amalgamate. Do not use a lot of flour either on the table or the rolling-pin, a mere dusting is enough.

QUICK PUFF PASTRY

125 grs (4 oz or $\frac{1}{2}$ cup) butter
250 grs (8 ozs or 2 cups) flour
$\frac{1}{2}$ teaspoon salt

4 raw yolks
7 tablespoons cold water
1 tablespoon lemon juice

Using a palette knife, cut the butter into the flour, add salt, continue to mix, incorporate yolks, water and lemon juice, work with the knife until the paste is smooth, then put on a lightly floured board. Roll out to a thickness of $\frac{3}{4}$ cm ($\frac{1}{4}$ inch), fold and leave to rest for 10 minutes. Repeat the rolling and folding process 3 times.

FINE CHOU PASTE

$\frac{1}{2}$ litre (1 pint or 2$\frac{1}{4}$ cups) water
pinch salt
1 tablespoon sugar
250 grs (8 oz or 1 cup) butter
220 grs (7$\frac{1}{2}$ oz or 2 cups) sifted flour

7–8 eggs (or 6–7 eggs and 4 tablespoons milk or cream)
1 tablespoon orange blossom water

Pour the water into a large saucepan with a thick bottom. Add salt, sugar and butter in small pieces, bring to a boil. Remove from heat and add flour, pouring it in all at once. Mix well. Cook, stirring with a wooden spoon, until paste comes away from the sides of the pan. Remove from heat and, stirring constantly, put in eggs one by one, then the milk or cream, if used. (The number of eggs used depends on their size.) The amount of milk indicated would replace one egg and make a smoother mixture. Flavour with orange blossom water.

Beat the mixture vigorously until it is very light.

TART PASTRY

375 grs (12 oz or 3 cups) **flour**
¼ teaspoon salt
1 teaspoon sugar (optional)

120 grs (4 oz or ½ cup) softened butter
water

Sift the flour, make a well in the centre and add salt, sugar and butter cut into pieces. Work the mixture together very quickly with your fingertips, adding just enough water to give a smooth pastry. If it is too soft, add a little flour. Rest several hours if possible before using.

FINE LINING PASTE

300 grs (10 oz or 1¼ cups) butter
500 grs (1 lb or 4 cups) sifted flour
1½ teaspoons salt

1 egg
1 teaspoon sugar
2–3 tablespoons milk

Knead the butter in a lightly floured cloth, coat it with 4 tablespoons flour and set aside. Spread remaining flour in a circle on a board, make a well in the middle, and put in all other ingredients, except butter. Knead until the dough becomes smooth and elastic. If necessary, moisten the fingers in a little water. Chill the dough for 10 minutes, then roll out and incorporate the butter. Roll in a ball and wrap in a lightly floured cloth. Refrigerate for 3 hours before using.

STRUDEL DOUGH

240 gr (8 oz or 2 cups) plain flour
½ teaspoon salt
1 beaten egg

1 dcl (1 gill or ½ cup) warm water
melted butter

183

Sift the flour and salt into a bowl four or five times. Make a well in the centre, add egg and water and mix with a fork to a very soft dough, adding a little more warm water, if necessary. Beat vigorously until dough pulls away from the side of the bowl. Turn out on to pastry-board and, with your fingers, lift, stretch, throw it against the board or pound with a rolling pin until it grows smooth and elastic, is not sticky and begins to 'blister' (about 15 to 20 minutes). This 'maltreatment' of the strudel dough is essential to ensure its elasticity for the stretching it has to do. Divide in two, roll into a ball, dust with flour, cover, and leave to 'rest' in a warm place for 45–50 minutes. Prepare the filling, for this must be ready before you start stretching the dough.

Put a clean cloth on a table, dust lightly with flour, put a ball of dough in centre, brush with melted butter and roll out slightly. Start to stretch the dough, pulling it with your hands. Gently stretch the dough in all directions, towards the edge of the table, working your way round until you have a dough that is tissue-paper thin, easing it carefully to prevent breaks. Tear off thick dough around edge. Let 'rest' again for 10 minutes. Brush with melted butter and spread with filling, keeping the dough on the cloth. Roll up into shape by lifting the cloth, pinch the edges to seal filling, trim off ends.

Place, sealed side down, on a baking sheet, brush with melted butter. Put in a moderately hot oven 205°C (400°F or Gas Mark 5) for 20 minutes, reduce heat to 175°C (350°F or Gas Mark 3) and continue to bake for a further 15–20 minutes, until crisp and pale golden.

FILO DOUGH

375 grs (12 oz or 3 cups) flour
½ teaspoon salt
2 teaspoons olive oil

about ¼ litre (½ pint or 1 cup) cold water
cornflour

Sift flour and salt into a bowl, add oil and enough water to make a stiff dough. Turn out on to a floured board and knead for 25–30 minutes to make the dough smooth and malleable. Dust with cornflour, cover with a cloth and leave to rest for 30 minutes. Divide into 12 pieces. Cover the table with a cloth and dust lightly with flour. Taking pieces of dough, pat with fingers, roll out as thinly as possible, then dust with cornflour and, working from the centre, stretch the dough towards the edges. (See Strudel Dough above). Continue until all 12 sheets are stretched paper thin.

Leave sheets of dough to dry slightly, for about 30–40 minutes. If you need to break off at this stage, the sheets of filo can be wrapped in waxed paper and kept in the refrigerator for a few hours.

CASES BAKED 'BLIND'

Roll out tart pastry, line a flan tin, press down gently, to make it fit and prevent formation of bubbles underneath, and crimp the edges. Prick the bottom of the flan all over with a fork, cover with a circle of greaseproof paper, cut to fit the bottom, and fill with dried beans or rice. Bake in a hot oven 205°C (400°F or Gas Mark 5) for about 30 minutes or until the flan case becomes lightly browned. (The beans can be stored and used again and again for the same purpose.)

PANCAKE BATTER

90 grs (3 oz or ¾ cup) flour	2 tablespoons cold water
pinch salt	2½ dcl (½ pint or 1 cup) milk
2 eggs	2 teaspoons melted butter

Beat flour, salt and eggs to mix well, gradually dilute with water and milk, incorporate melted butter, stir until the batter is smooth and creamy, and chill until needed. Stir well before using.

BATTER FOR CRÊPES

360 ml (¾ pint or 1½ cups) milk	4 tablespoons sugar
300 grs (10 oz or 2½ cups) sifted flour	240 grs (8 oz or 1 cup) butter
4 egg yolks	4 egg whites, beaten stiff

Blend the milk and flour in a bowl with a whisk. Add yolks, stirring well until blended. Add sugar and stir again. Melt the butter in a double boiler and pour it into the mixture. Fold in the beaten egg whites and mix well.

NOODLE PASTE

240 grs (8 oz or 2 cups) flour	2 yolks
7½ grs (¼ oz or 1½ teaspoons) salt	cold water
2 whole eggs, lightly beaten	

Sift the flour and salt, add eggs and yolks and enough cold water to make a firm paste. Roll, fold twice, allow to rest for an hour before using.

To make noodles, fold paste sheets into rolls and with a sharp knife cut into strips.

DOUGH FOR SAMOSAS

6 Servings

180 grs (6 oz or 1½ cups) flour
  (plain)
salt
4 tablespoons ghee (or clarified
  butter (p. 219)

120 ml (4 oz or ½ cup) curds or
  yoghurt

Sift flour and a pinch of salt into a bowl, stir in ghee and the curds, knead gently into a dough, roll into a ball, cover with a bowl and leave to stand for 25–30 minutes.

Creams, Fillings, Butters

CRÈME PATISSIÈRE, CONFECTIONERS' CUSTARD OR FRENCH PASTRY CREAM

1 litre (2 pints or 4 cups) milk
½ kg (1 lb or 2 cups) sugar
120 grs (4 oz or 1 cup) sifted flour
pinch salt
12 egg yolks
1–2 tablespoons melted butter
a few drops vanilla flavouring

Bring milk to the boiling point. Mix remaining ingredients together. Little by little, add the milk. Blend well. Put into a double boiler and simmer for a few minutes, stirring constantly. Turn out into a bowl and gloss the top with melted butter.

Note : In addition to vanilla, this cream can be flavoured with coffee, cocoa, grated orange or lemon rind. (The latter should be put into the milk before heating.)

CREAM SAINT-HONORÉ

15 gr (½ oz or 1 envelope)
  gelatine
½ litre (1 pint or 2 cups) confectioners' custard (above)
6 egg whites
60 grs (2 oz or ¼ cup) sugar

Soften gelatine in 60 ml (2 oz or ¼ cup) cold water for 15 minutes.

Prepare confectioners' custard. When the cream is cooked, remove from heat and add gelatine. Beat egg whites very stiff, adding sugar during the last few minutes of beating. While cream is still hot, slowly fold in egg whites. Serve at once.

ALMOND CREAM

240 grs (8 oz or 1¼ cups) almonds
240 grs (8 oz or 1 cup) sugar
5–6 egg yolks
240 grs (8 oz or 1 cup) melted butter
1 teaspoon vanilla flavoured sugar
  (p. 113)
1 tablespoon rum

Blanch the almonds by putting them into a sieve and plunging into a saucepan of boiling water for 2 minutes. Drain the almonds as soon as the skin comes off when pressed with the fingers. Skin them quickly, rinse in cold water, drain and dry.

Pound the almonds in a mortar, add sugar; add the eggs one by one; and finally, add melted butter. Continue pounding until the mixture is reduced to a smooth paste, scraping the walls of the mortar from time to time. Put into a bowl and mix in vanilla flavoured sugar and rum.

Another method : to ½ litre (1 pint or 2 cups) of confectioners custard (p. 187), add above quantity of pounded almonds, sugar and butter.

BUTTER COFFEE CREAM

240 grs (8 oz or 1 cup) sugar
6 egg yolks
240 ml (8 oz or 1 cup) strong
    coffee

360 grs (12 oz or 1½ cups) butter

Cream sugar and yolks until the mixture is light and smooth. Little by little, add hot strained coffee. Put in the top of a double boiler over gentle heat and, stirring constantly, cook until the mixture begins to thicken and approaches boiling point. As soon as it coats the spoon, remove from heat and strain into a bowl.

When the custard has cooled a little, incorporate butter, added in small pieces. Blend in first with a spoon, then whisk vigorously. The whisking action will make the mixture smooth, creamy and shiny. Use at once without letting it get cold, as this will cause the cream to harden.

FRANGIPANE CREAM

1 litre (1 quart or 4½ cups) milk
1 vanilla bean
240 grs (8 oz or 2 cups) sifted
    flour
½ kg (1 lb or 2 cups) castor sugar

pinch salt
4 whole eggs
6 egg yolks
120 grs (4 oz or ½ cup) butter
4 tablespoons crushed macaroons

Bring the milk to a boil with vanilla bean. Put flour, sugar, and salt into a bowl, mix, and dilute with eggs and egg yolks. Little by little stir the hot, strained milk into this mixture. Pour the mixture into the top of a double boiler and heat almost to boiling point, stirring constantly. Remove from heat, add butter and finely crushed macaroons.

188

Pour the frangipane cream into a bowl, stirring with a wooden spoon until cold to prevent formation of a skin, or dab the surface of the cream with a piece of butter spiked on a fork.

CHANTILLY OR WHIPPED CREAM

½ litre (1 pint or 2 cups) double cream
4–5 tablespoons sugar

1 teaspoon vanilla sugar (p. 113)
or
¼ teaspoon vanilla extract

The above ingredients will make one litre (one quart) of whipped cream. The cream should be very cold for whipping. Put it into a basin and beat until it doubles its volume and forms peaks. Carefully fold in sugar and serve.

CREAM CHEESE FILLING

480 grs (1 lb or 2 cups) cream cheese
1 dcl (1 gill or ½ cup) double cream
2 teaspoon flour
4 beaten eggs

pinch salt
¼ teaspoon pepper (opt)
30 grs (1 oz or 2 tablespoons) butter
sugar to taste

Combine cheese, cream, flour, eggs, salt, sugar and pepper. Blend in butter. Use as filling for cheesecake, tarts, etc.

ORANGE BUTTER FOR CRÈPES SUZETTE

90 grs (3 oz or 6 tablespoons) unsalted butter
6–8 lumps orange sugar (p. 217–8)

2 tablespoons Grand Marnier or Curacao

Combine all ingredients and blend well.

BRANDY BUTTER

250 grs (8 oz or 1 cup) unsalted butter
250 grs (8 oz or 1 cup) castor sugar

6 tablespoons brandy

Cream butter; sift in sugar, beating all the time until white and fluffy. Drip in brandy, stirring well. Spoon into a pretty serving dish. Chill well before serving.

This 'hard sauce', as the Americans call it, will keep for a fortnight in a covered jar in the refrigerator.

RUM BUTTER

As for Brandy Butter, substituting rum for brandy.

Icings

CHOCOLATE BUTTER ICING

90 grs (3 oz or ¾ cup) grated
    chocolate
1 tablespoon **milk**
a few drops vanilla essence

2 tablespoons brandy (optional)
240 grs (8 oz or 1 cup) butter
180 grs (6 oz or 1¼ cups) icing
    sugar

Melt chocolate with milk, vanilla and brandy, stirring it over simmering water.

Cream butter, sift the sugar into it and beat.

Cool the chocolate slightly, without allowing it to set, stir into butter and sugar mixture, whisk hard until the icing is smoothly blended and use as required.

CHOCOLATE BUTTER ICING FOR SACHERTORTE

120 grs (4 oz or ⅔ cup) plain
    chocolate
75 grs (2½ oz or ⅓ cup) butter
105 gr (3½ oz or ¾ cup) icing
    sugar

pinch salt
3 egg yolks

In the top of a double boiler, melt chocolate. Allow to cool.

Cream butter, sugar and salt together until light and fluffy. Add the egg yolks, one at a time, beating well after each one. Slowly add the cooled melted chocolate, blending well.

FONDANT ICING

240 grs (8 oz or 1 cup) sifted
    confectioners' sugar
2 tablespoons milk

¼ teaspoon almond or vanilla
    extract

Mix all ingredients until smooth.

Dessert Sauces

APRICOT SAUCE

½ litre (1 pint or 2 **cups**) apricot jam (p. 213)
240 ml (½ pint or 1 **cup**) water

60 grs (2 oz or ¼ cup) sugar
Kirsch or Maraschino
a few drops vanilla essence

Put all the ingredients into a pan, boil gently for 5 minutes, skim, and strain, rubbing the fruit through. Keep hot in double boiler. At the last moment, flavour to taste with Kirsch or Maraschino and vanilla.

STRAWBERRY OR REDCURRANT SAUCE

Follow recipe for Apricot Sauce, using strawberry or redcurrant jam, flavoured with Kirsch.

RASPBERRY SAUCE

Follow recipe for Apricot Sauce, using raspberry jam flavoured with Maraschino.

CRANBERRY SAUCE FOR STEAMED PUDDING

120 grs (4 oz or 1 cup) cranberries
120 grs (4 oz or ½ cup) sugar

¼ litre (½ pint or 1 cup) cream, whipped (p. 189)

In the top of a double boiler, cook cranberries and sugar until fruit is soft. Rub through a sieve and when cool, fold in lightly whipped cream.

SULTANA SAUCE

150 grs (5 oz or 1 cup) sultanas
1 tablespoon sugar
240 ml (½ pint or 1 cup) water

1 dessertspoon cornflour
120 ml (1 gill or ½ cup) sherry

Boil the sultanas with the sugar in the water until they are plump and tender. Blend cornflour with sherry and stir into the sauce. Simmer until it thickens, stirring all the time.

RUM SAUCE

2 raw yolks
3 tablespoons sugar
120 ml (4 oz or ½ cup) water

strained juice or 1 lemon
1 wineglass rum

Whisk yolks with sugar, gradually dilute with water, stir well and pour the mixture into a double saucepan (or cook in a bain-marie). Add lemon juice and rum, simmer gently, without allowing to boil, until the sauce thickens.

RED WINE SAUCE

1 teaspoon potato flour
120 ml (4 oz or ½ cup) water
120 ml (4 oz or ½ cup) sweet red wine

120 gr (4 oz or ½ cup) sugar
2 raw yolks
lemon juice

Dilute potato flour in 2 tablespoons cold water. Put the rest of the water, red wine and sugar in a pan and gently bring to the boil. Stir to make sure sugar is completely dissolved. Blend in diluted potato flour. Have a double saucepan ready on the simmer. Drop the yolks into it, little by little add the wine sauce to them, whisking all the time. Simmer gently in a double saucepan (or bain-marie) until the liaison thickens the sauce.

PRALINE SAUCE

Mix 1 litre (2 pints or 4 cups) of Custard Cream (p. 15) with 3 tablespoons finely pounded, blanched and burnt almonds, hazel nuts or pistachio nuts.

CHOCOLATE SAUCE

120 grs (4 oz or 1 cup) grated semi-sweet chocolate
5 tablespoons water

240 ml (½pint or 1 cup) cream
2 tablespoons butter

Cook the chocolate with water over low heat for 15 minutes, stirring from time to time. Just before using, remove from heat, add cream and butter. Whisk vigorously for two minutes and serve.

AMERICAN CHOCOLATE MARSHMALLOW SAUCE FOR ICE CREAM

½ kg (1 lb) marshmallows   250 ml (½pint or 1 cup) cream
½ kg (1 lb) plain chocolate

Cut marshmallows into small pieces. Shave chocolate and place in the top of a double boiler with the marshmallows and cream. Place over simmering water and stir frequently until all is dissolved. This amount will make 3½ cups sauce. It will keep in a covered jar in refrigerator.

Candy, Sweetmeats

MEMBRILLO

1 kg (2 lb) quinces	sugar
120 ml (¼ pint or ½ cup) water	icing sugar

Wash and cut up the quinces. Stew them in water until soft. Pass them through a sieve, weigh or measure the resulting purée and put it into a saucepan with equal amount of sugar. Boil gently, stirring all the time, until the mixture leaves the side of the saucepan. Pour into dishes lined with greaseproof paper and set in a warm place to dry off for two or three days. We find ice cube trays a good shape for this. Cut into long strips, about 2½ cm (1 inch) thick, roll in icing sugar. Wrap in greaseproof paper and store in an airtight tin.

Eat these slices with salty hard goat's cheese, or cottage cheese, or nibble on its own. In Spain membrillo is traditionally eaten with Manchego cheese. Membrillo is also eaten with cheese in Argentina and is known there as Postre del Vigilante (Policeman's Dessert).

INGBER/CARROT CANDY

This is one of the traditional Jewish sweetmeats served during Passover. The quantities given below should make about 30 pieces of ingber.

1 kg (2 lb) carrots	180 grs (6 oz or 1½ cups) blanched,
½ kg (1 lb or 2 cups) sugar	chopped almonds
1½ teaspoon ground ginger	sugar for final sprinkling
3–4 tablespoons lemon juice	

Scrape the carrots, rinse and grate finely. Put in a saucepan with sugar and cook over an asbestos mat on a very low heat, stirring frequently. As soon as sugar is dissolved, add ginger and lemon juice and continue to cook gently, stirring, until all moisture evaporates and the mixture is thick. Stir in nuts and remove from heat.

Spread on a board sprinkled with sugar, sprinkle the surface with a little sugar, allow to cool, then, before the candy sets hard, with a knife mark into squares.

Leave until quite cold and hard, break into marked out pieces.

KOREAN DATE SWEETMEATS

6 Servings
750 grs (1½ lb) dates	1 teaspoon cinnamon
3 tablespoons sugar	60 grs (2 oz or ½ cup) pine nuts

Wipe the dates with a cloth, stone and steam for 15 minutes to soften. Rub through a sieve or pass through a blender. Stir in sugar and cinnamon, mix well. Chop the pine nuts finely. If pine nuts are not available, use blanched almonds.

Taking a teaspoon of the date purée at a time, shape into balls, roll in pine nuts and arrange on small individual dishes.

These are typically oriental sweetmeats, served as a special dinner dessert or as something for the ladies to nibble at tea-time. In the Middle East they are often decorated with blanched slivered almonds, crushed cardamom seeds, silver balls, silver hundreds and thousands; in India, for a festive occasion, they are wrapped in silver leaf.

COCONUT DELIGHTS

¾ litre (1½ pints or 3½ cups) milk	120 gr (8 oz or ½ cup) sugar
120 gr (4 oz or 1⅓ cups) finely grated coconut	butter
	nutmeg
2–3 tablespoons shredded coconut	edible silver leaf (optional)

Slowly bring the milk to the boil, add both kinds of coconut and simmer for 25–30 minutes. Add sugar and continue to simmer until all surplus moisture is evaporated and the mixture is thick. Spread it evenly in a lightly buttered shallow dish, sprinkle with freshly grated nutmeg and leave until cold. Cut into lozenges and cover with a film of silver leaf.

KOREAN CHESTNUT BALLS

6 Servings

750 grs (1½ lb) chestnuts
1 teaspoon ground ginger
1 teaspoon ground cinnamon
90 grs (3 oz or 6 tablespoons)
   sugar

60 grs (2 oz or ½ cup) pine nuts
   (or blanched almonds)
180 grs (6 oz or ½ cup) honey

Make a light incision around each chestnut and cook in enough boiling water to cover for 15 minutes. Drain, cool, remove shell and skin. Mash the chestnuts or pass through a blender to obtain a smooth purée. Add ginger, cinnamon and sugar and mix well. Chop pine nuts roughly. Taking a teaspoon of chestnut purée at a time, shape into uniform balls, dip in honey to coat the surface completely, roll in chopped pine nuts, pressing gently to make them adhere, correct shape if necessary and arrange on a serving dish.

JALEBIS

Jalebis are sometimes sprinkled with ground pistachio nuts, after soaking in syrup, and can be served either hot or cold. Jalebi powder is used as colouring and can be bought in shops specialising in Indian ingredients. If not available, use saffron or turmeric.

180 gr (6 oz or 1½ cups) flour
¾ tablespoon baking powder
3 tablespoons curds or yoghurt
water
½ kg (1 lb or 2 cups) sugar

1 teaspoon jalebi powder
a few drops rose or jasmine
   essence
ghee or oil for deep frying

Sift the flour and baking powder into a bowl, gradually dilute by adding 2½ dcl (½ pint or 1 cup) warm water, stir in curds and leave the batter in a warm place to ferment overnight.

Dissolve sugar in 1 dcl (¼ pint or ½ cup) water, add jalebi colouring and flower essence, boil until the syrup thickens, remove from heat and keep warm, over hot water. Heat ghee or oil until it begins to bubble.

Beat the batter, if necessary add more flour or water to make sure the batter has the consistency of double cream. Pour the batter into the boiling ghee through a funnel, moving the funnel in such a way as to form rings within rings. As soon as one spiral is done, close the funnel with your finger, and repeat the pouring to make the next jalebi.

Fry only a few at a time, to prevent sticking, until golden brown on both sides. Remove with a perforated spoon, drain off fat and plunge into warm syrup.

Leave in the syrup for 15 minutes to allow the jalebis to absorb it.

Drain and arrange on a shallow dish.

CINNAMON BALLS

4 Servings

2 egg whites	1 level tablespoon cinnamon
120 grs (4 oz or ½ cup) castor sugar	icing sugar
240 grs (8 oz or 2⅔ cups) ground almonds	

Beat the whites until stiff. Fold in all the rest of the ingredients. Moisten hands and make the mixture into small balls. Put on a greased flat tin, making sure to leave a space around each. Pre-heat oven to 175°C (350°F or Gas Mark 3). Bake for 25 minutes or just until they are firm to the touch but do not overbake. Roll them in icing sugar when *warm* and again when *cold*.

DATES STUFFED WITH ALMOND PASTE

480 gr (1 lb or 2 cups) wiped, pitted dates	1 tablespoon vanilla sugar (p. 113)
240 gr (8 oz or 1½ cups) shelled almonds	1 raw egg yolk
240 gr (8 oz or 1 cup) castor sugar	1 tablespoon anis liqueur
135 gr (4½ oz or 1 cup) icing sugar	a few drops colouring matter (optional)

Wipe the dates, slit with a knife down one side and remove the pit.

Blanch the almonds, i.e. scald them with boiling water and slip off the skins. Dry on a cloth.

Mince the almonds with castor sugar, pound in a mortar or pass through a blender, to make a smooth paste.

Blend the yolk with half the icing sugar and the vanilla sugar, stirring well until creamy. (By hand this operation takes 15 minutes). Add liqueur, stir well and blend this cream into the almond paste. Add colouring, if desired.

Using a little of the paste at a time, roll into pellets about twice the size of the pits, and stuff the dates. Roll in remaining icing sugar and decorate with a pattern traced with a knife.

Kirsch or rum are also excellent as flavouring for the almond paste.

LOUKOUM (Turkish Delight)

¾ kilo (1½ lb or 3 cups) castor
sugar
½ litre (1 pint or 1 cup) water
4 tablespoons cornflour
6 tablespoons white grape juice
1 teaspoon cream of tartar
1 tablespoon rose water

3 tablespoons shelled pistachio
nuts
a few drops cochineal
1 tablespoon almond oil
90 gr (3 oz or 1 cup) ground
coconut
120 gr (4 oz or ⅞ cup) icing sugar

Put castor sugar and water in a pan and slowly bring to the boil, then simmer gently until the sugar is dissolved. Dilute cornflour with grape juice and gradually blend into the syrup. Add cream of tartar and continue to cook slowly, stirring all the time, until the mixture thickens. Remove from heat, add rose water and pistachio nuts.

Divide the mixture in two; leave one half plain and colour the second with a few drops of cochineal.

Grease a couple of shallow tins with almond oil. Pour the white mixture into one tin and the pink into the other. Leave to set and cool completely.

With a sharp knife cut into squares. Dip the white loukoum in ground coconut, making it adhere on all sides. Roll the pink loukoum in icing sugar.

COCONUT PYRAMIDS

180 gr (6 oz or 2½ cups) desiccated
coconut
120 gr (4 oz or ½ cup) sugar

30 gr (1 oz or 3 tablespoons) potato
flour
3 egg whites

Pre-heat oven to 177°C (350°F or Gas Mark 3).
Combine coconut, sugar and potato flour.
Whisk the egg whites until very stiff and fold into coconut mixture. Put mixture on a lightly greased baking sheet in spoonfuls, work into pyramid shapes and bake for 35–40 minutes until crisp and lightly coloured.

HONEY AND POPPY SEED CANDY

360 gr (12 oz or 1 cup) honey
360 gr (12 oz or 2¼ cups) poppy
seeds

1 tablespoon lemon juice
180 gr (6 oz or 1 cup) blanched
almonds

Heat honey until it melts, add poppy seeds and lemon juice and slowly bring to the boil. Add almonds and, stirring from time to time, continue to cook until the syrupy mixture reaches the soft ball stage. To test, drop a spoonful into a cup of cold water. The right degree is reached if the mixture has a consistency which can be moulded into a soft ball with the fingers.

Professional confectioners use a saccharometer and the soft ball is registered at 110°C–116°C (230°F–240°F). Remove from heat and continue to stir for a few minutes. Spread the mixture in an even layer (1¼ cm or ½ inch thick) on a moistened slab or board, cut into diamond shapes and leave to harden. Store in air-tight jars or tins.

For complete success in making this sweetmeat, it is essential to cook the syrup to the right degree, and to make sure that the almonds are thoroughly dry before they are added to honey and poppy seeds.

MARZIPAN

240 grs (8 oz or 1⅓ cup) blanched sweet almonds
water
4 or 5 bitter almonds

½ kg (1 lb or 2 cups) castor sugar
a few drops orange flower water
extra castor sugar
rice paper

Pound the almonds in a mortar, moistening from time to time with a little water, until they are reduced to a smooth, rather stiff paste. Transfer into a heavy bottomed saucepan, add sugar and orange flower water. Stir with a wooden spoon, over a low flame, until the mixture is thoroughly dried. Return to the mortar and work with the pestle until the paste becomes very smooth. To make it even smoother, knead the paste by hand, on a marble slab. Roll the paste out to a thickness of 1½ cm (⅔ inch). Put it on a sheet of rice paper and cut into little squares, hearts, leaves, or whatever you like. Put these shapes on a baking sheet covered with greaseproof paper and dry in a very cool oven 120°C (250°F or Gas Mark ½).

The finished paste will keep for a long time in the refrigerator. For decorations: roll out on to a sugared marble slab (no rice paper).

I find the best way to make leaves look like real leaves, is to cut each one separately by hand, not using a pastry cutter, because that makes them all look too much alike, then with a fine point (a pin, or a wooden toothpick) to draw in the veins. I slightly curl the edges of some of my leaves. I prefer my marzipan uncoloured, but the addition of a little green vegetable colouring, or cochineal, before you return the paste to the mortar, will give you spring and autumn bouquets. Be sparing with colourings, or your finished effect will not look good enough to eat.

Marzipan can also be rolled or kneaded into shape.

To make cob nuts, wrap a little, uneven, finely rolled out piece of paste round one end of an egg shaped lump of marzipan. With scissors, cut the edges of the wrapper to look as much like the real thing as possible, and join two 'nuts' together at the base. Dry for a couple of hours in a very cool oven 120°C (250°F or Gas Mark ½). (T.L.)

GAJJAR HALVA/CARROT HALVA

½ kg (1 lb) carrots
1 litre (1 quart) milk
2 tablespoons honey or golden
 syrup
180 grs (6 oz) sugar
pinch ($\frac{1}{16}$ teaspoon) saffron

1 teaspoon crushed cardamom
 seeds
pinch salt
2 tablespoons sultanas
butter
roasted chopped almonds

Scrape and grate the carrots. Bring the milk slowly to the boil, add carrots and simmer gently for 30 minutes, stirring frequently.

Add honey, sugar, saffron, cardamom, salt, sultanas and 3 tablespoons butter. Blend well and continue to cook over lowest possible heat for another 30–40 minutes until all moisture is evaporated and the halva begins to look very solid and deep orange in colour. Remove from heat, spread evenly in a lightly buttered shallow dish, cool, sprinkle with almonds and chill. To serve, cut into squares.

Crystallised Fruit, Candied Berries, etc.

CANDIED ORANGE PEEL (OR LEMON PEEL)

240 grs (8 oz or 2⅔ cups) orange peel
7½ grs (¼ oz or 2¼ teaspoons) bicarbonate of soda

360 grs (12 oz or 1½ cups) sugar
water

Wash the oranges, cut them in half and carefully remove all the pulp and pith. Slice the peel into convenient size strips 7½ cm (3 inches long and 1¼ cm (½ inch wide. Weigh or measure to obtain specified amount.

Dissolve bicarbonate of soda in 1 litre (2 pints or 4 cups) boiling water and soak the peel in this for quarter of an hour. Drain, rinse in cold water, and put the peel in a pan of fresh water to cover and cook until tender and drain. Using 240 grs (8 oz or 1 cup) sugar and ¼ litre (½ pint or 1 cup) water, make a light syrup (p. 217). Put peel into syrup. Cover and leave for two days. Drain off syrup, add remaining sugar to the peel, heat and simmer the peel until it is transparent. Drain off syrup again and put peel on wire rack to dry, with a tray underneath it, in a cool oven, at its lowest setting. Boil up remaining syrup until very dense. Remove the dried peel from the oven and dip each piece in the dense syrup before returning to the oven to dry off again.

Use for decoration, or to nibble on.

Store in an airtight jar.

CHOCOLATE ORANGE PEEL

Prepare and dry orange peel as described above. Dip one end of the strips of peel in melted chocolate and cool on a sheet of aluminium foil.

Serve with strong black coffee.

MEXICAN CRYSTALLISED LIME SHELLS

I first ate these in Guadalajara, with flame trees in the courtyard, at a restaurant patronised by rich ranchers whose beef I much enjoyed before the limes. They are delicious, the lime having such a subtle flavour.

For special occasions, used crystallised lime shells as cups for lime water ice. Do not refrigerate cups. Fill them with ice just before serving. (T.L.)

12 limes	water
360 grs (12 oz or 1½ cups) sugar	
7½ grs (¼ oz or 2½ teaspoons) bicarbonate of soda	

Wash and halve limes. Scoop out all the pulp, leaving little 'cups of lime rind. Proceed as for candied orange peel (p. 205). To dry, place the 'cups' neatly, upside down, to keep their shape.

To make lime water ice, use fresh lime juice and follow recipe for Orange Sorbet (p. 171).

MOROCCAN CANDIED CHESTNUTS

Good edible chestnuts flourish in the Mediterranean region and are used in many ways, from soups to desserts. Chestnuts have a very high food value and innumerable ways of preserving them have been evolved, but this recipe is perhaps the most satisfying of all. All you need to turn them into marrons glacés is to wrap them in metal foil.

1 kg (2 lb) chestnuts	1 vanilla bean
1 kg (2 lb or 4 cups) castor sugar	1 stick cinnamon
1 litre (1 quart) water	

Score the chestnuts, bring to the boil, simmer for 30 minutes, remove shell and inner skin and put in a bowl.

Warm sugar, heat gently with water, vanilla and cinnamon. Simmer and stir to dissolve sugar completely. Pour syrup over chestnuts, cover and leave overnight.

On the following day, drain off syrup into a pan, bring to the boil and remove vanilla bean (which can be washed, dried and used again). Discard cinnamon.

Put chestnuts in a preserving pan, pour syrup over them and leave to stand for 4 hours. Place an asbestos mat under the pan, heat gently, and simmer on lowest possible heat for 2 hours without allowing syrup to boil. Remove chestnuts carefully with a perforated spoon, letting the syrup drip off the pan and put them in jars.

Re-heat syrup and boil it down to concentrate and thicken. Pour over chestnuts, allow to cool in jars and seal.

Leave for 3–4 weeks. Drain chestnuts carefully, without breaking them. Bring syrup to the boil, put chestnuts into it, remove from heat and leave to complete the candying process for 15 minutes. Drain chestnuts, place on cake rack to dry off, and they are ready for eating or to be given away as treats.

MEBOS / AFRICAANS APRICOTS

480 grs (1 lb or 3 cups) dried
  apricots
480 grs (1 lb or 2 cups) sugar

$\frac{1}{4}$ teaspoon salt
icing sugar

Soak the apricots overnight. The next morning, strain, mince and add sugar. Stir over heat until sugar melts. Add salt and continue to cook until the mixture reaches setting point. Test by dropping a little of the mixture into a glass of cold water. As soon as it sets in the water, it is ready.

Spread the apricot mixture on a sugared board, flatten to a thickness of $1\frac{1}{4}$ cm ($\frac{1}{2}$ inch). Cut into desired shapes and sprinkle with icing sugar.

HONEYED GRAPES

4 Servings
  $\frac{1}{2}$ kg (1 lb or $2\frac{1}{2}$ cups) seedless
    grapes
  1 teaspoon lemon juice
  90 grs (3 oz or 4 tablespoons)
    honey

2 tablespoons sherry (or brandy)
sour cream (optional)

Wash grapes and remove stems.

Combine lemon juice, honey and sherry and pour over the grapes.

Chill for several hours or preferably overnight. Decant into dessert glasses, top with sour cream and serve.

CANDIED REDCURRANTS

Mix one white of egg with 240 grs (6 oz or 1 cup) of sifted sugar, add a tablespoon of lemon juice, stir with a wooden spoon until the mixture turns white and thickens. Dip clusters of redcurrants into this icing, make sure that all the berries are properly coated, put on a lightly greased tray and dry off the glaze either in a very slow oven or in the open.

REDCURRANTS IN PETTICOATS

Dip clusters of redcurrants into white of egg, roll in sifted sugar, lay on lightly buttered baking tray and put in a very slow oven, 135°C (275°F or Gas Mark 1), to dry. Redcurrants served this way are delicious but do not keep.

FROSTED FRUITS

(These will not keep for more than a couple of hours.)

Suggested fruit:	strawberries
grapes	1 egg white
redcurrants (I like this best T.L.)	icing sugar
blackcurrants	

Select only the best looking fruit, wash and dry carefully. Leave the stalks on. Brush the fruit with lightly beaten egg white. Dredge with icing sugar. Leave on a paper towel to harden.

Nibblers

NUT BRITTLE

makes ¾ kg (1½ lbs) candy
½ kg (1 lb or 2⅔ cups) blanched
  almonds (hazelnuts, walnuts,
  etc.)

½ kg (1 lb or 2 cups) sugar
pinch salt
water
1 teaspoon cinnamon (optional)

Roast nuts in the oven until they are golden brown. Cool. Spread on a sheet of aluminium foil.

In a heavy bottomed pan, add enough water to the sugar and salt just to moisten the sugar without making it very wet. Heat until the sugar is dissolved and the resulting syrup has turned a fine caramel brown. Pour over the nuts, dust with cinnamon. When cool, break into bite-sized pieces.

Variation: Use sesame seeds, pine kernels, melon seeds.

CINNAMON ALMONDS

½ kg (1 lb or 2⅔ cups) almonds
1 egg white

120 grs (4 oz or ½ cup) sugar
60 grs (2 oz) cinnamon powder

Remove the almond skins by immersing for 5 minutes in boiling water. Dry them. Dip them in the stiffly beaten egg white and roll them in the sugar mixed with cinnamon. Put them in a large enough baking tin to hold them without crowding them. Bake in the oven pre-heated to 135°C (275°F or Gas Mark 1) for about an hour. Cool.

ALMOND CRUNCH

480 grs (1 lb or 2½ cups) blanched
  almonds
240 grs (8 oz or ⅔ cup) honey

240 grs (8 oz or 1 cup) castor
  sugar
1 teaspoon ground cinnamon

Make sure the almonds are thoroughly dry.

In a heavy skillet gently heat honey and sugar. Add almonds, sprinkle with cinnamon and cook on low heat until the almonds turn a pale brown and the sugar reaches the hard ball degree (p. 217).

Stir, remove from heat, spread out to cool in an even layer, cut into uniform square pieces and store in airtight tins.

SPICED ALMONDS

240 grs (8 oz or 1¼ cups) icing
   sugar
2½ tablespoons cornflour
1 teaspoon cinnamon
¼ teaspoon ground cloves
¼ teaspoon ground allspice

¼ teaspoon ground chilli
½ teaspoon salt
2 egg whites
3 tablespoons water
375 gr (12 oz or 2 cups) blanched
   almonds

Combine sugar, cornflour, all the spices and salt. Beat egg whites with water.

Heat oven to 120°C (250°F or Gas Mark ½).

Dip a few almonds at a time in egg white and roll in spiced sugar making sure it adheres in an even coating. Put almonds on a baking sheet without allowing them to touch, bake for 1½–1¾ hours. When cold, put in airtight tin until required.

TAYGLACH

This is a Jewish confection, made of dough, boiled in ginger-flavoured honey or golden syrup and rolled in chopped nuts or desiccated coconut. The quantities given in this recipe should produce about 3 dozen tayglach.

240 grs (8 oz or 2 cups) self-raising
   flour
small pinch salt
2 teaspoons ground ginger

2 large eggs
½ kg (1 lb or or 1½ cups) honey
240 grs (8 oz or 2 cups) chopped
   almonds (or other nuts)

Sift the flour with salt and ½ teaspoon ginger. Beat the eggs lightly and add to flour, mix and knead dough until smooth. Roll into thin rolls 1¼ cm (½ inch) in diameter and cut into 1¼ cm (½ inch) pieces.

Melt honey with remaining 1½ teaspoons ginger and bring to the boil. Drop the pieces of dough into boiling honey, a few at a time, no more than a dozen. As soon as boiling is re-established, reduce heat and boil gently for 25–30 minutes. The tayglach should be a pale biscuit colour. Do not stir during cooking.

Moisten a board, sprinkle with chopped nuts. Remove tayglach from honey with a perforated spoon, put on the board and spread evenly with a wet wooden spoon. Cool and cut into uniform pieces or shape into little pyramids and leave to dry.

Jams and Preserves

APRICOT JAM

Peel and pit ripe apricots. Reserve pits. For 250 grs (8 oz 1 cup) apricots allow 180 grs (6 oz ¾ cup) sugar and 2 tablespoons water. Put the sugar in a pan with the water. Let the sugar dissolve. Bring to a boil and add apricots. Cook on a fairly high flame, stirring all the time until the jelling stage is reached. Test frequently. As soon as the drops come together on edge of the spoon and slide off as one drop, the jam is ready, 105°C (220°F) on the sugar thermometer. At the last moment, add shelled, blanched and halved apricot kernels from about one-third of the apricots. Pour into sterilized jars and seal.

ROSE PETAL JAM

500 grs (1 lb) fresh red rose petals
boiling water
iced water

500 grs (1 lb) lemons
500 grs (1 lb or 2 cups) sugar
1–2 drops rose oil

Pick petals of newly opened roses, trim off white parts and measure out 500 grs (1 lb) petals. Put in collander, scald with boiling water, pressing the petals gently with a spoon, if they tend to float up. Drain and plunge collander into iced water, with ice cubes in it. Repeat this operation of scalding and plunging into iced water once more. This will make the petals crisp and crunchy in the jam. Drain well.

Peel lemons, cut into quarters and then slice very thinly. Put into pan, add 120 ml (4 oz or ½ cup) water, bring to the boil, simmer to soften.

Warm sugar, put in a pan with 2 tablespoons water, simmer, stir to dissolve. Add lemons, rose petals and rose oil, boil until the jam begins to set. Start testing after 3 minutes.

This jam is used for a very special Persian rice pudding which is flavoured with rose water and decorated with fresh roses.

REDCURRANT JELLY

1 kg (2 lb or 8 cups) redcurrants   sugar
¼ litre (½ pint or 1 cup) water

Simmer red currants with water until the skins break. Hang in thick muslin or a jelly bag over a bowl to catch the juice and leave to drip overnight.

Measure the juice and pour into preserving pan. For each 500 ml (1 pint or 2 cups) of juice add 500 grs (1 lb or 2 cups) sugar. Stir it until dissolved completely. Boil until jelling point is reached. Start testing after 6–7 minutes.

OLD ENGLISH MINCEMEAT

375 grs (12 oz or 2¼ cups) stoned raisins	480 grs (1 lb or 2 cups) demerara sugar
240 grs (8 oz or 1 cup) minced candied peel (p. 205)	rind and juice of 1 lemon
500 grs (1 lb) peeled, cored apples	rind and juice of 1 orange
240 grs (8 oz or 1 cup) sultanas	1 teaspoon ground cloves
240 grs (8 oz or 1 cup) currants	1 teaspoon ground nutmeg
240 grs (8 oz or 1 cup) chopped suet	1 small bottle of barley wine (strong ale)
	2 tablespoons brandy

Mix all the ingredients together, stir well and leave in a covered bowl for a week, stirring each day. Put in sterilised jars, seal and store. Use as required.

Note : We are often asked why this mixture of currants, raisins, apples, etc., is called mincemeat. The reason is that meat used to be an ingredient. Gradually the amount of meat was reduced and now the only trace of it in English mincemeat is the suet.

Cooked beef or venison is used in American mincemeat. In Canada green tomatoes are included in the ingredients.

Mincemeat is essential for mince pies, which a French historian of English cookery described as 'legendary table mate of plum pudding. Its absence from a Christmas dinner would be looked upon as a breach of tradition'.

Mincemeat can also be used as filling for fritters, pancakes and dessert omelettes.

MINT CHUTNEY

This refreshing chutney needs no cooking but it does not keep and should be made fresh on the day on which it is to be used. If mango is not available, use equivalent amount of fresh lime or lemon juice.

60 grs (2 oz) mint leaves	1 teaspoon sugar
8 spring onions (opt)	1 teaspoon garam-masala (p. 219)
2 small fresh green chillies	1 tablespoon pomegranate seeds
pinch salt	2 tablespoons sieved mango pulp

Wash and chop mint leaves. Chop spring onions and chillies. Pound the mint, spring onion, chillies, with salt, sugar and garam-masala in a mortar. Crush pomegranate seeds, add to mixture and continue to pound together for a few minutes. Stir in mango, mix well, decant into a serving dish.

Miscellaneous

BASIC SYRUP

Five degrees of basic syrup are used in the preparation of sweets at home. There are more, but these will suffice in an ordinary home kitchen. All are made in the same way and differ only in the time of cooking and in the proportion of sugar and water. The less water used, naturally, the thicker the syrup.

First degree syrup is a light one – if tested on a spoon it is just a little tacky.

Second degree syrup – is slightly thicker, cooked a bit longer and if tapped with a spoon, forms a fibrous thread.

Third degree syrup – can be tested by dropping a spoonful into a cup of cold water. It should be of a consistency that can be moulded into a soft ball with the fingers.

Fourth degree is a thick syrup – a spoonful dropped into cold water will solidify into a firm brittle ball with air bubbles in it.

Fifth – is caramel. It needs little water, just enough to moisten the sugar – and should be cooked until it is golden. Always use an aluminium pan and a wooden spoon for making syrup. Correct proportions of sugar and water are given in individual recipes.

To caramelise a dish or mould, i.e., coat it with sugar cooked to caramel degree (fifth), proceed as follows: heat several pieces of sugar moistened with a little water in the mould itself, until the syrup acquires a brown colour. Then rotate the mould so as to coat its inside evenly. Alternatively, brush the interior of a mould or dish with sugar cooked to caramel degree.

ORANGE OR LEMON SUGAR

To make orange or lemon sugar, rub the fruit with a sugar lump until it is completely covered with the rind. Scrape off and use this coloured surface. Repeat the operation until enough flavoured sugar is obtained.

PRALINE (Almond paste) I

120 grs (4 oz or ½ cup) sugar
1 teaspoon vanilla extract

90 grs (3 oz or ½ cup) blanched
almonds

Put sugar and vanilla into a pan, melt over a good heat until sugar browns.

Roast the almonds in the oven to brown them, add to sugar, and mix together.

Pour on to a greased plate to cool, then pound in a mortar as fine as possible.

To make cream praline, add praline to custard cream.

PRALINE II

120 grs (4 oz or ½ cup) sugar
half pod vanilla, or 1 teaspoon
  vanilla extract
  water

135 grs (3½ oz or ¾ cup) almonds,
  blanched and browned in the

Put sugar and vanilla in a heavy bottomed pan. Melt over a good heat until it is brown. Add almonds, mix well, pour into a greased baking tin, cool, then pound in a mortar as finely as possible.

COCONUT CREAM AND MILK

To make coconut cream:

1 fresh coconut
120 ml (4 oz or ½–1 cup) boiling water

Have the greengrocer saw the coconut in half, pour out the liquid. (The natural, and drinkable, liquid inside the coconut is *not* coconut milk.) Extract the flesh, by scraping it out. Pour boiling water over it and let it stand for 20 minutes. Squeeze out in a muslin bag or pass through a fine strainer. This first pressing produces coconut cream, which after several hours' refrigeration acquires the density of double cream.

To make Coconut milk:

Put the husks of the coconut which has been pressed to extract cream into a pan, add the same amount of water as for the first pressing, bring to the boil and press out again. Both coconut cream and milk can be made in a liquidiser. Observe the indicated proportions, and blend a couple of tablespoonfuls of grated or shredded coconut and water at a time. Then squeeze through a muslin bag as described. If fresh coconut is not available good quality desiccated coconut may be used.

CLARIFIED BUTTER

Melt the butter on a very low heat until it begins to look like olive oil and a whitish deposit forms on the bottom of the pan. Strain into a clean container and use as directed.

GARAM-MASALA

60 grs (2 oz or $\frac{1}{2}$ cup) coriander seeds
60 grs (2 oz or $\frac{1}{2}$ cup) black peppercorns
45 grs (1$\frac{1}{2}$ oz or 6 tablespoons) caraway seeds

15 grs ($\frac{1}{2}$ oz or 6 tablespoons) cloves
20 peeled cardamom seeds
15 grs ($\frac{1}{2}$ oz or 2 tablespoons) ground cinnamon

Mix all ingredients and grind. A coffee grinder does this job very well and the final product should be fine but not reduced to dust. Store in a jar with a well-fitting lid. Garam-masala is an essential ingredient in most curry dishes.

BARLEY WATER

60 grs (2 oz or 5 tablespoons) barley
2 litres (4 pints or 8 cups) water

peel of $\frac{1}{2}$ lemon (in strips)
sugar to taste

Barley is one of the oldest cultivated cereals which still exists in its original form.

Barley water was one of the most popular medicines used by Hippocrates, who prescribed it 'with or without grains, depending on nature of malady'.

Barley water is very refreshing and in country districts is still used to comfort an upset stomach. It is also said to be very good for the kidneys. Our reason for including it is that it makes truly delicious Lemon Barley Cream (p. 45).

Wash pearl barley thoroughly. Bring to the boil in water with lemon peel, cook until liquid is reduced by half. Allow to stand for a moment, strain through muslin, pressing well and sweeten with sugar to taste.

KAYMAK

Kaymak is Turkish clotted cream, much appreciated through-out the Middle East, the Caucasus and in Russia. There is no substitute for it and labour involved in making it is well worth the trouble.

Being a cooked cream, kaymak keeps for several days in a refrigerator. It is different in texture from Devonshire clotted cream. Kaymak is skimmed off in layers, which are rolled up and when cold can be cut into portions.

To turn ½ litre (1 pint or 2 cups) of single cream into kaymak may take up to 40–45 minutes. You must heat it to boiling point gently, then taking up a ladleful at a time, pour it back into the pan to make the bubbles rise high. This is important, for the higher you get the bubbles to rise, the more kaymak you will have. Remove from heat, cover, leave to stand undisturbed for 2 hours, then chill overnight.

On the following day, with a sharp knife loosen the bubbles of cream, which by now should be very firm. Roll up layers of this thick clotted cream, like a skin.

Cut into portions and serve with ekmek kadayif (p. 92), baklava (p. 91) and fruit.

GLOSSARY

BABA – A kugelhupf-type cake, made of leavened dough, steeped in Kirsch or rum after cooking. The invention of this is credited to King Stanislas Leczinski, who was reputed to be a fervent reader of the *Thousand and One Nights* and named the cake after Ali Baba.

BAIN-MARIE – Vessel containing hot water in which sauces, custards, etc., can be cooked or kept hot without coming into contact with direct source of heat. The temperature of water in a bain-marie should be kept near boiling point.

To BAKE BLIND – to bake a pastry case before adding filling.

BARQUETTES – Small boat-shaped tartlets.

To BLANCH – To dip food for a minute in boiling water, then plunge in cold water, to make peeling easier. (Peaches, almonds.)

To CARAMELISE – To melt sugar in a heavy pan, stirring, until it forms a dark brown syrup. To coat moulds, etc., with this syrup.

CREAM OF TARTAR – Raising agent in cookery, an ingredient of baking powder.

CURDS – Coagulated part of milk. To make quickly, add 1 teaspoon of lime or lemon juice to ¼ litre (½ pint or 1 cup) lukewarm milk.

To DREDGE – To sprinkle with flour or sugar.

ECLAIRS – Small pastry made of chou paste (see recipe p. 89).

To FOLD IN – To mix beaten mixtures (especially whites of egg or cream) so that they don't lose their lightness.

GARAM-MASALA – A mixture of ground spices, essential ingredient of all curry dishes.

GHEE – Clarified butter, originally made from buffalo milk, used in Indian cookery and available in tins.

GUGELHUPF – see Kugelhupf.

KANTEN – Agar-agar, seaweed gelatine, used for Japanese sweets.

KUGELHUPF (p. 83) – Alsatian pastry, a favourite of Marie Antoinette's. Carême is said to have introduced it to Paris, having been given the recipe by the Austrian Ambassador. In France, first of April Kugelhupf is baked in a fish-shaped mould and coated with chocolate, to look like poisson d'avril.

To PUREE – To rub cooked fruit, etc., through a sieve or pass through a blender.

Index

223

227